The Oldest House in Hadley. Erected in 1713

Historic Hadley

A STORY OF
THE MAKING OF
A FAMOUS MASSACHUSETTS TOWN

Alice Morehouse Walker

HERITAGE BOOKS
2007

HERITAGE BOOKS
AN IMPRINT OF HERITAGE BOOKS, INC.

Books, CDs, and more—Worldwide

For our listing of thousands of titles see our website
at
www.HeritageBooks.com

A Facsimile Reprint
Published 2007 by
HERITAGE BOOKS, INC.
Publishing Division
65 East Main Street
Westminster, Maryland 21157-5026

Copyright © 1906 The Grafton Press
New York

— Publisher's Notice —
In reprints such as this, it is often not possible to remove blemishes from the original. We feel the contents of this book warrant its reissue despite these blemishes and hope you will agree and read it with pleasure.

International Standard Book Number: 978-0-7884-1397-1

Copyright, 1906,
By THE GRAFTON PRESS.

TO

THE SOLDIERS AND STATESMEN, PROFESSIONAL MEN AND LAYMEN, TILLERS OF THE SOIL AND PRODUCERS OF WEALTH AND WELL-BEING SCATTERED THROUGHOUT MANY STATES AND RESIDENT IN FOREIGN PARTS, DESCENDANTS ALL OF THOSE FIRST SETTLERS WHO FOUNDED HADLEY AMID THE MEADOWS OF THE WINDING CONNECTICUT MORE THAN TWO CENTURIES AGO, THIS SIMPLE STORY OF GREAT DEEDS IS DEDICATED.

FOREWORD

LOVE of one's own town is one of the dominant motives underlying good citizenship. The origin, growth, and development of a typical New England town, covering two centuries and a half, is a theme on which any thoughtful person may profitably dwell. In these busy days, however, few people have the time necessary to read a ponderous volume. For the many rather than the few this little book has been written.

The lands of the early settlers of Hadley are passing into the possession of the children of aliens, and the town-meeting, church, school, and homes are for these strangers to control. This book is for these also, that they may be imbued with the spirit of those mighty souls, which remains still potent enough to make Americans out of Europeans, even as in 1776 it made patriots and freemen out of the subjects of King George.

In the endeavor to make these pages interesting and to impart to them the fascination of a story, truth has not been sacrificed to style. Painstaking effort has been made to search the town records, to scrutinize every historical document, and to weigh carefully familiar traditions. The old dwellings, the highways and byways, the mountains, the river and the meadows, the ancient elms, heirlooms and antique relics have been questioned and cross-questioned until they have broken their silence of centuries and told the story of by-gone days.

The author acknowledges with pleasure the help derived from the study of the voluminous manuscripts of Sylvester Judd, now carefully guarded in the Forbes Library in Northampton, and his "History of Hadley," completed after his death by the late Lucius M. Boltwood. Credit should also be given for the aid afforded by "The History of the Hopkins Fund," prepared and published under the direction of the Trustees of Hopkins Academy. "The History of Western Massachusetts," by J. G. Holland, has elucidated some interesting points of the narrative.

It is hoped that this volume will be read and re-read, and that copies will be sent with the best wishes of the senders to distant friends, that all the world may be familiar with Historic Hadley, sitting by the riverside, the mother of towns, of churches, and of schools.

A. M. W.

AMHERST, MASS., July 4, 1906.

CONTENTS

CHAPTER I

THE FOUNDERS AND THEIR FORTUNES 1

The Indian Owners of the Quonektacut Valley. The "Engagers." The Emigration. Establishing the New Town. The First Winter in "Norwottuck Beyond Springfield." Laying Out the Broad Street. The Meadows and the Plains. Varied Duties of the New Settlers. Origin of the Name Hadley. Parson John Russell and His Work. Joseph Kellogg and His Ferry. Building the Meeting-house. Home Lots on the Broad Street. Extension of the Town Limits. Death of Governor Webster. Doctor John Westcarr. Hadley Dames Presented in Court for Wearing Silk. Secession of the "West Siders." Preparation for Trials to Come.

CHAPTER II

A REIGN OF TERROR IN OLD HADLEY 22

General Edward Whalley and General William Goffe, Fugitives from the High Court of Justice. Parson Russell's Hospitality. News of King Philip's Uprising. The Hampshire Troop of Horsemen. The Ambuscade near the Indian Fort. The Attack. The Angel Sent from God. Days of Terror. Death of Captain Lothrop near Muddy Brook. Burning of Springfield. Hopeless Condition of Hadley. The Winter of 1675 and 1676. Preparing for a Siege. Building the Palisades. Death of Deacon Goodman and Captivity of Thomas Reed. The "Falls Fight." Friendly Indian Allies. The Parade of the Army from Connecticut on Hadley Street. Feeding the Swarm of Soldiers. The Attack on Hadley, June 12, 1676. The "Great Gun." Superstitious Terrors. Mary Webster, the Witch. Death of Parson Russell.

x   Contents

CHAPTER III

THE CHURCH IN OLD HADLEY 40

I.—*The Pastorate of Rev. Isaac Chauncey*

Securing the New Pastor. Murder of Richard Church by Indians. Discovery and Punishment of the Murderers. Controversy Regarding the Seating of the Meeting-house. Effect of the Peace of Utrecht. Removing the Fortifications. The Arts of Peace. Building the Second Meeting-house. Later Repairs and Renovations. Church Manners and Customs. Slavery in Hadley. Joshua Boston and Arthur Prutt, Two Hadley Slaves. The Sad Story of Cæsar Prutt. Selling a Slave at Amherst Town-meeting. The Extraordinary Adventure of Zebulon Prutt. Establishment of the Southern Precinct Beyond the Mountain. Setting Off the East Precinct. The Interrupted Career of Israel Chauncey. Activity of Parson Chauncey and His Final Retirement.

II.—*The Pastorates of Rev. Chester Williams and Dr. Samuel Hopkins*

Prosperity in Hadley. Parson Williams' Wardrobe. Jonathan Edwards and His Controversy. Appointment of the Hadley Minister as Scribe of the Council of Churches. Sickness and Death of Parson Williams. Ordination of Rev. Samuel Hopkins. His Marriage to Mrs. Chester Williams. The "Awful Earthquake" in Hadley. Home of Captain Moses Porter. His Call to Duty, and Death in the Battle of Lake George. Burial of Madam Porter. Personality of Rev. Samuel Hopkins. Burning of the Pastor's House. A Presage of Revolution. The Call to Arms. News of the Battle of Lexington. The Porter Family in Old Hadley. The Porter Homestead, the Oldest House in Hadley. Colonel Elisha Porter's Call to Quebec. Return of Part of Burgoyne's Army to Hadley. Hospitality of Colonel Porter. The Sword of Burgoyne. Hadley Soldiers in the Revolution. Shays' Rebellion. General Lincoln with His Army in Hadley. Preaching to the Soldiers from Behind a Pulpit of Snow. Planning the Third Meeting-house. Dedication of the New Building.

III.—*Rev. John Woodbridge and His Successors*

Death and Burial of Dr. Hopkins. Rev. John Woodbridge. Visit of President Timothy Dwight. Moving the Meeting-house. Division in the Church. The Withdrawal from the First Church and the Establishment of the Russell Church. Successors of Rev. Mr. Woodbridge. The Old Church To-day.

Contents   xi

CHAPTER IV

HOPKINS GRAMMAR SCHOOL AND ACADEMY   . .   74

Early Ideas Concerning Schools. Parson Russell's Desire. Governor Edward Hopkins and His Will. Trustees of the Will. The Hadley Trustees of the Grammar School. The Hadley School Meadows, and the Committee in Charge. First Teaching in Hadley. Caleb Watson and His School. School Regulations. Early Hadley Teaching. The First Schoolhouse. Investment of the Funds. The School Mill. Departure of Ruling Elder Goodwin, and His Suit Against the Trustees. Burning of the Mill During the War. Efforts to Make the School an English School. Opposition of Parson Russell to the Scheme. Town-meeting at Break of Day. Re-establishment of the Grammar School. The New School Committee. Josiah Pierce, the Schoolmaster Who Raised Potatoes. The Brick Academy Building. Later Preceptors of Hopkins Academy. Decline of the Academy. The Free High School. Burning of the Academy Building. Sale of School Lands and of the Mill Site. Graduates and Former Students of Hopkins Grammar School and Academy.

CHAPTER V

THE WEALTH OF THE RIVER AND THE FERTILE
  MEADOWS   98

The Connecticut River in Olden Time. The Indians and the River. Pines Along the Bank. Influence of the River on the Early Settlements. Floods. Shad and Salmon. The Fishery at the "Greate Falls." Lumbering in the Valley Towns. Trouble on Account of Logs. Rafting. The Lumber Road and the Saw Mills. Traffic on the River. The "Great Canoes." The Falls Boats. The Proprietors of the Locks and Canals. Digging a Canal Around the Great Falls. Planting Elms in Hadley Street. A New Kind of "Corn Seed." The Broom Corn Industry. The First Steamboats on the River. The Coming of the Barnet. A Voyage on the Vermont. The Steamboat William Hall Plying Between Hadley and Hartford. A Picnic on the Franklin. The Railroad to Springfield from Northampton. Railroad Connection with Boston. Connecting Electric Trolley Lines. Passing of the Romance of the River.

CHAPTER VI

THE BURIAL PLACE OF HADLEY'S HONORED DEAD 117

First Burial on the Meadow Plain. Burial of Governor John Webster. The Old Hadley Cemetery. Inscription on the Webster Monument. Death and Burial of Each of the Founders. Rude Gravestones on the Older Graves. Burial of Hadley Slaves. Early Funeral Fashions. The Earliest Monuments Marking the Graves of Parson Russell and His Wife. Inscriptions on These Stones. Stones Marking the Graves of the Other Ministers. Grave of Bishop Frederic D. Huntington.

ILLUSTRATIONS

The Oldest House in Hadley. (Built in 1713.) (See p. 63.)
Frontispiece

	FACING PAGE
Old Hadley Street To-day (looking south from Russell Street)	14
The Meadow Plain and the Holyoke Mountains (looking southeast from the river)	22
The Present Hadley Meeting-house. (Built in 1808 and moved to its present site in 1840)	40
Hopkins Academy Building. (Built in 1894)	74
The Connecticut River and the Meadow Plain (looking north from the railroad)	98
Old Hadley Burying Ground	117

HISTORIC HADLEY

HISTORIC HADLEY

CHAPTER I

THE FOUNDERS AND THEIR FORTUNES

THE Indian owners of the valley bordering on Quonektacut, the "Great River," were very desirous that the English should settle in their midst. These lordly hunters scorned the thought of labor, and their toiling squaws were able to cultivate but a small portion of the fertile openings between the groups of pines and cedars. The white man, after the bargain was completed, would be willing that his red brothers should hunt in his forests and fish in his streams, and for his meadow land would pay long strings of wampum, coats and breeches, guns and ammunition, brass kettles, knives and needles, with perhaps a taste of the fiery drink known as "kill devil" to seal the bargain.

The Puritan members of the churches in Hartford and Wethersfield differed among themselves concerning baptism. Therefore the minority in each congregation withdrew from its communion, and, encouraged by Parson Russell of Wethersfield, commissioned Major John Pynchon, the famous trader, to buy for them a portion of the Massachusetts wilderness where in peace they might practise and believe. The old chieftains Chickwallopp, Umpanchala, and Quonquont were ready to sell their ancient heritage, and the Connecticut "withdrawers" were anxious to buy. The bargain, therefore, was soon concluded; each red man made his mark upon the deed; and the land from Mount Holyoke on the south, to Mount Toby and Mohawk Brook on the north, and extending eastward nine miles into the woods, passed into the possession of Major Pynchon, and was by him transferred to the "withdrawers," who termed themselves "Strict Congregationalists," and adhered to the good old doctrines and opposed all new-fangled notions in preaching and practise. The "withdrawers," by this historic act transformed into the "engagers," at a meeting held April 18, 1659, in Hartford, in the home of Goodman Ward, signed an agreement to "remove themselves and their families out of the jurisdiction of Conecticut into the jurisdiction of the Mattachusets." They also appointed William Westwood, Richard Goodman, William Lewis, John White, and Nathaniel Dickinson "to go up to the aforesaid plantation and lay out 59 homelots." Most of the signers of this agreement had never seen the place which was to become their home.

Many of these "engagers" were men of wealth and learning, holding responsible positions which they were willing to relinquish for conscience's sake. Among the leaders was the Honorable John Webster, a former governor of Connecticut and one of the Commissioners of the United Colonies, who had been deeply interested in the controversy of the churches. He died in Hadley when the town was still in its infancy. His daughter Elizabeth married William Markham, one of the "engagers," and Anne, another daughter, became the wife of John Marsh, whose name also is on the list. John Russell, Sr., a glazier by trade, cast his fortunes with his son, Parson John Russell, the leader of the Wethersfield contingent, and signed the agreement. Lieutenant Samuel Smith, a "man of note," also was an "engager," and was foremost among the promoters of the embryo settlement. These all appear among the Hadley pioneers, the real founders of the town. Others, less constant in their purpose, allowed their signatures to stand, but carried their projects no farther.

The journey from Hartford northward into the wilderness was beset with difficulty. The "Greate Falls" prevented transportation by water and the Holyoke mountains stood squarely across the most direct pathway by land. Undaunted, however, a few of the "engagers" packed their household goods in ox carts, made nests for their children among the feather beds, mounted each his wife behind him on a pillion, and thus plodded along the rugged cart-way to Windsor, and thence through Waranoke, now Westfield, toward Northampton, the new town which was to be their western neighbor. Crossing the river in canoes, they pitched their tents until cabins could be built for temporary homes.

Once arrived at their destination, these energetic and methodical pioneers determined that from the first everything should be done decently and in order. November 9, 1659, they called a town-meeting, and appointed a committee of seven "to order all public occasions that concern the good of the plantation for the Yeare Insuing." This committee made a "rate" to pay the minister's salary, and sent messengers to Hartford and Wethersfield that those "engagers" who had not removed might not fail to contribute their share. The town was laid out on both sides of the river, Richard Fellows being the first settler on the west side. He was followed by Thomas Meekins, William Allis, Nathaniel Dickinson, Jr., Thomas Graves and his sons Isaac and John, Samuel Belding, Stephen Taylor, John White, Jr., Daniel Warner, Richard Billing, Zachariah Field, Daniel White, John Cowls, Samuel Dickinson, and John Coleman. Before 1661 these had built their homes on what is now Hatfield Street, then known as the "West Side." Among the settlers who established themselves on the east side of the river were the townsmen: William Westwood, Nathaniel Dickinson, Samuel Smith, Thomas Standley, John White, Richard Goodman, and Nathaniel Ward. Exactly what other families may have been there we cannot tell. Lest there should be jealousy it was voted that "All that sett down on the land on the west side of the river shall be one with those on the east side, both in ecclesiastical and civil matters," and for several years both "siders" made strenuous efforts to make good this action of the town.

And so came into being the nameless settlement in the wilderness of "Norwottuck beyond Springfield." We can readily imagine the difficulties which must have beset the colonists during that first winter of 1659 and 1660. Overlooking the southern meadow was an Indian fort from which the few small houses in Northampton could be seen. Toward the north the chieftain Quonquont and his tribe lived in their wigwams beside the river. The idle, thriftless Indians were friendly neighbors, upon whom the settlers must have depended for favors without end. The native hunter drove many a sharp bargain with his white brother for corn and maple sugar, taking pay in ammunition, knives, and needles which could not well be spared from the white man's scanty store, while the squaw for a consideration furnished moccasons and deerskins ready dressed, from which warm clothing was made. Thus protected from the cold the heads of families and elder sons were obliged to hunt on the mountains and fish through the ice to secure sufficient daily food. With energetic strokes the choppers felled great pine trees and cleared the underbrush in preparation for the other "engagers" who might come in the spring. The woods were full of howling wild beasts, and wolves nightly prowled around the clearing. Where now we see the wide and level street, there then were ridges and hollows and ponds. That winter must have been a season of arduous toil, and with the spring came the great floods which caused the hearts of the newcomers to fail within them.

With perseverance, however, the pioneers laid out their broad highway, twenty rods in width, bordered with home lots of eight acres each. This street extended across the peninsula, with the "Greate River" for its boundary at either end. Samuel Smith and Peter Tilton measured and staked the lots for threepence per acre, and caused the name of each proprietor to be placed upon his stake. He was then required to enclose his own lot by a fence made of five rails fastened to posts four feet high. Another way of fencing was to dig a ditch three feet wide and two feet deep and throw the earth upon one bank, on which a fence of three rails was set. Every man was obliged to labor on the fences at the ends of the street and at the west end of the "laines" running into the woods, at each of which there was to be maintained a "Goode Gaite."

The vast eastern forests were known as the "Woods" or the "Pine Plain," and the western and southern grazing lands constituted the "Greate Meadowe," within whose boundary lines was the "Forlorn Hope." The little "Aqua Vitæ" meadow bordered the river near the home of the ferryman, Joseph Kellogg. In 1663 Hockanum meadow was divided and ordered to be fenced by its owners. Each person was obliged to keep his cattle on his own part of the meadow, on penalty of twelvepence fine for every "hoge" or "shoate," and one shilling eightpence for a "score of sheepe" that should go astray. The sharp eyes of the hayward, Goodman Richard Montague, were always on the lookout for offenders, as he received a percentage on all fines collected. Viewers of fences were men of importance in those days, as upon their faithfulness depended the welfare of the little hamlet. Almost before the fences were built William Westwood and Thomas Standley were chosen to perform that duty. Each person had "plow land" and "moeing land" in the "Greate Meadowe," and some living in the south part of the town were given shares in Fort Meadow, its swamp being accounted "two for one." To see that these cultivated fields, upon the products of which the very existence of the settlement depended, were not disturbed by the droves of young horses and cattle which roamed on the mountains and through the woods required constant care of many miles of fencing.

In addition to service for the public welfare, each farmer was compelled at first to be his own carpenter and blacksmith, and to grind his own corn, and make his own bolts, and "pailes" and clapboards and shingles. He was ordered by the town fathers, after felling any "rift timber" (oak) or any "pine tree," to make it at once into needed articles, on penalty of having it confiscated by any one who chose to take it. Those of the settlers who, like Nathaniel Dickinson, had several lusty sons to share their toil must have been envied by others who were wholly dependent for assistance upon neighbors and the few who were willing to work for wages.

The citizens of the "Newtown," as the settlement was sometimes called, had now secured their hearts' desire for freedom from controversy with regard to the "half way covenant," but they had no meeting-house, and did not possess even a legal name. Those among the Hartford men who came from Essex, in England, were glad to christen their new home Hadleigh, or Hadley, dear to their youthful hearts in days gone by, and in 1661 this action was confirmed by the General Court in Boston.

John Russell, Jr., the minister of Wethersfield, who with a portion of his flock had already cast his lot with the "engagers," was willing to accept the formal call to build up a church among a united people. His father had secured an allotment of land on Hadley street, and his brother Philip was one of the settlers on the "West Side." The parson, John Jr., was graduated from Harvard College in 1645 when nineteen years of age, preached in Wethersfield about ten years, and probably came to Hadley in 1660. In that year the "Said Inhabitants and Planters" voted to pay him eighty pounds annual salary, and gave him a home lot of eight acres next to the middle highway leading to the woods. The minister had to build his own house and clear his own land. No mention is made of any provision by the people of firewood for his use. So in order that his wife and three little children should not freeze, the minister was obliged to chop down trees and draw them to his own dooryard. At first he had no servants, and the three negro slaves included in the inventory of his estate were probably bought years later when family cares had increased. Parson Russell's salary was paid in winter wheat at three shillings threepence, peas at two shillings sixpence, and Indian corn at two shillings per bushel, all of which commodities had to be exchanged for other goods as there was little money. But though obliged to perform much manual labor, the minister was not required to offer prayer at funerals, or to officiate at weddings, the latter duty being performed by the justice of the peace. No doubt the magistrate united the minister himself first to Mary Talcott, then to Rebecca, daughter of Thomas

Newbury of Windsor, and again to Phebe, widow of Rev. John Whiting of Hartford. Rebecca, the wife who came with Parson Russell to Hadley, is buried by his side in the old Hadley cemetery.

Jonathan Russell, the son of the minister, was for twenty-eight years pastor of the church in Barnstable, and Samuel, another son, was the minister in Branford, Connecticut. These two, and John, the first born son, who died when young, were inmates of that new Hadley home. William Westwood, the first local magistrate authorized to unite couples in marriage, pronounced his own daughter Sarah and Aaron Cooke husband and wife, after which they doubtless partook of "sack posset" by way of a mild celebration after the good old fashion. This was the first wedding in Hadley. Parson Russell did not perform a marriage ceremony in Hadley until just before his death.

The newly appointed minister preached his first sermon in a private house, for, in spite of their best efforts, the settlers could not build a meeting-house that first year. December 12, 1661, we find the statement in the records: "The Town have ordered that they will Build and erect A meeting house to be a place for publick worship, whose figure is 45 foote in length, and 24 foote in Bredth, with Leantors on both sides, which shall Inlarge the whole to 36 in Bredth." "This shall be scittuated and sett up on the common street." But other matters were so pressing that it seems to have taken them long to build the Lord's house, and probably during this time meetings were held in the home of some leading church member.

The people, however, were not idle, for public affairs demanded much attention. Joseph Kellogg, the first ferryman, had built his house on the ferry lot at the south end of the street, where he received as fares eightpence in wheat, or sixpence in money, for man and horse. On lecture days, when six or more persons went together, the rate was decreased, and after dark the fares were doubled. The ferryman was also allowed to keep an "ordinary" and entertain strangers. Lieutenant Joseph, who afterward became the father of twenty children, had quite a family even now, and with his ferry passengers and guests he for one could not have had much time to assist in building the meeting-house. The town had to aid Parson Russell in the work of putting an addition on his dwelling, and then at his request engaged William Goodwin as an elder to assist him in his work. Part of the parish being across the river there must have been times when two men were absolutely required to look after manners and morals according to the rigid standard of that day. Many town-meetings were held, for absence from which penalties were imposed on busy men. The farmers held chopping bees and felled great trees in such a manner as to form bridges over the smaller brooks, and built a more elaborate bridge for horses, oxen, and carts across Fort River on the Springfield road, and contributed toward the expense of laying out a "commodious way to the Bay." Wearied with the labor of grinding their grain in their own homes they offered Goodman Meekins a fifty-pound allotment on the west side of the "Greate River" upon which to build a mill, the citizens agreeing to patronize him so long as he made good meal. Thomas Wells and John Hubbard were appointed to carry the corn in a boat across the river twice a week, and to bring back the meal, for which they should receive threepence a bushel, each farmer to have his corn ready and his bags marked with his name. Finally a sawmill was erected on Mill River, thus making it less difficult to get out lumber.

Again the citizens brought up the matter of building the meeting-house, and on August 27, 1663, in town-meeting assembled, passed the following resolution: "The town have voted (nemine contradicente) that they will with all convenient speede, endeavour and set aboute the building and erecting a meeting house for publick worshipp." The following committee was put in charge: William Clarke, Samuel Smith, William Westwood, John Barnard, Thomas Meekins, Nathaniel Dickinson, and Isaac Graves. The work at last was started and this time the attempt was a success, although the building was not completed for seven years. The construction of the "Leantors" was abandoned and there is every reason to believe that the house as first used conformed in other respects to the original plan. According to the vote the building was "scittuated and sett up in the common street," toward the north, in order to accommodate residents on the "West Side." The solid framework was put together and, after delay, was raised, but the building was not then completed, possibly because the western settlers had already begun to discuss plans for having a meeting-house and minister of their own.

Great was the alarm at the thought of the desertion of the "West Siders," for the whole parish found it difficult to raise enough grain with which to pay Parson Russell's salary. Should the western part of the parish secede, taking with it the corn mill, the settlement would be crippled indeed! There seems to have been some discussion in regard to moving the half-finished meeting-house, for the vote stands to the effect: "Untill the Lord makes it appear that one part of us have a call to make a society of themselves," they would remain united and let the meeting-house stand "in or about the place where it was wrought and framed." Thus referring the matter to the Lord, they proceeded with the work, and soon the little building, similar in fashion to the one in Hartford, was firmly set upon its hill, that it might not be hid. Above its solid frame rose a sloping roof, alike on all four sides, with probably a turret in the middle for the bell which they hoped soon to secure. The committee then collected the roughly hewn "Boards and Rales" from the individuals by whom they had been prepared, and made long benches without backs, and a rude pulpit, after which they rested to await developments.

A stranger coming into Hadley from the south, in 1663, would cross the river on Joseph Kellogg's ferry-boat, and would possibly take dinner with him and his numerous family in the ferry-house at the Aqua Vitæ meadow. The settlement at this time was laid out on both sides of the broad street which extended north and south across the eastern part of the peninsula made by the river in its detour westward toward Northampton. The land enclosed between the street and the river on the west was the fertile Meadow Plain. To the east stretched the vast Pine Plain or Woods. Leading away westward from the street were three highways, known respectively as the north, middle, and south highway to the meadow, and three similar highways led from the main street eastward toward the woods. At the extreme southeastern corner of the settlement, on the southern side of the south highway to the woods, lived John Russell, Sr., father of the minister. Nathaniel Dickinson, and his son Thomas Dickinson, lived in the same section of the town on the eastern side of the street and north of the south highway. Next in the line on the east side of

OLD HADLEY STREET

the street was the house of William Westwood, in the midst of his eight-acre lot, where he lived with his wife, Bridget, and daughter, Sarah, who married Aaron Cooke. Then came the home of Richard Goodman and his wife, Mary Terry of Windsor, and infant son, John. Others who lived on the east side of the street in the southeastern section were: William Lewis, who in 1662 represented Hadley in the General Court; the Hon. Peter Tilton, recorder, representative, associate judge of the county court, and "one of the most worshipful assistants of the colony"; John White, also a representative; Thomas Stanley, and Nathaniel Stanley, his son; Andrew Bacon; and John Barnard, afterward slain by the Indians.

In the northeastern section of the settlement, on the east side of the street, just north of the middle highway to the woods, lived Parson Russell, and immediately north was the town lot. North of the town lot on the east side of the street were the homes of John Hubbard, Thomas Wells, Samuel Porter of Windsor, whose son Samuel became judge and sheriff of the county and the father of thirteen children; John Dickinson, the son of Nathaniel; Richard Montague, the grave-digger; Lieut. Samuel Smith, a "man of note"; and his son Philip Smith, who was afterwards slain by the machinations of the witch Mary Webster; Thomas Coleman; and William Partrigg. Next on the north lived A. Nichols, John Ingram, John Taylor, and Wm. Pixley.

In the northwestern quarter of the settlement, north of the northern highway to the meadow, lived Samuel Gardner. South of the northern highway and on the western side of the street lived Chileab Smith, son of Lieutenant Samuel Smith; Joseph Baldwin; Robert Boltwood; Francis Barnard, father of John Barnard; John Hawkes; Richard Church; and Edward Church, his son. South of the middle highway and on the western side of the street were the homes of Henry Clark, "a wealthy and distinguished man"; Stephen Terry; Andrew Warner; John Marsh; Timothy Nash, the blacksmith; Governor John Webster; William Goodwin; John Crow; Samuel Moody; Nathaniel Ward; and William Markham, who married Elizabeth, the daughter of Governor Webster.

The unfinished meeting-house stood in the middle of the broad street about opposite the house of John Dickinson, somewhat to the north of the middle highway. All about it up and down the broad street were the homes of these founders of Hadley, heroic men, imbued with the spirit of the Pilgrims and the courage of their convictions. The innumerable company of their descendants, scattered abroad throughout the earth, are proud to trace their ancestry back to the pioneer settlers of this famous New England town. The visitor would have seen small, unpretentious dwellings, a rough unpainted meeting-house, and signs of a rude colonial life. But he would have found the dwellers in these homes to be men of education and refinement, and women of energy and determination, bringing up their children in the fear of God and with a wholesome respect for man. Out of such material was this nation builded.

Exactly when the congregation left the private house and began to worship in the church building we cannot tell, but probably as soon as the seats were finished. Perched in the pulpit high against the wall, good Parson Russell looked down upon his flock, and discussed and determined doctrinal points to the satisfaction of all concerned. The town voted to buy a bell "brought up by Lieut. Smith and some other," and to pay for it in wheat at three shillings per bushel, which amounted to about twenty-five dollars. Finding its feeble tones were scarcely heard across the river, and fearing lest the "West Siders" would recognize in this grievance the looked for sign of a call from the Lord, a parishioner left in his will a sum of money with which to buy a larger bell, that might be heard generally by the inhabitants. At last a committee was chosen "to procure such a bell as is at Northampton," which proves that the Hadley people were progressive and not to be outdone by the town on the other side of the river.

Pending this action the lusty bell-ringer, standing

in the audience room, pulled the rope which came down through the ceiling, and strained the voice of the little bell to its utmost, as he summoned the faithful to the Sunday service. Across the river in boats, and from north and south on foot, on horseback, and in rude carts, they came, fathers and brothers well armed, though in time of peace, and mothers with their younger children, through summer's heat and winter's cold, to sit on the hard benches through the long and tedious service. It seems a significant fact that two years after the galleries were put into the meeting-house the town passed the vote which has been so many times quoted: "that there shall be some sticks set up in the meeting-house, in several places, with some fit persons placed by them, to use them as occasion shall require to keep the youth from disorder."

The Indians, too, were scattered throughout the congregation, and greeted the settlers with the friendly salutation "Netop" and were seeming converts to the Christian faith; and yet the shrewd old-time fathers felt it wise not to trust them too far even on Sunday, and appointed special guards for the Lord's day, and for lectures and public meetings for God's worship. The citizens were organized into a military company for which the townsmen procured a drum, and thus in time of peace prepared for war.

Attempts were made to clear the highways of pine trees, logs, woodpiles, and "other encumbrances" which had collected in front of the houses. The town voted "their desire of John Prentice of New London to come and sitt amongst them as a smith," and offered him the "lott sequestered for a smith." When he declined they opened communication with Deacon Hinsdale at the Bay "for a Smith then living in roxberrie."

Before the meeting-house was finished it was considered to be the center of the town, for, taking the building as an objective point, in 1663 the General Court decided that Hadley should extend five miles up the river, five miles down the river, and four miles from the most eastern point of the river. Those who were dependent upon their cattle and grain to pay their living expenses urged that they needed more extended pastures, as much of their feeding-ground was barren pine plain. After a time they were given land extending two more miles to the east, and the meadows to the south.

In 1670 the settlers on the west side of the river, assured at last that the Lord had called them to become a separate town, left their former brethren, and built for themselves a meeting-house on their own broad street. This was a blow to Hadley by which Parson Russell lost some of his best supporters. Valuable members of the church had also been removed by death. The remains of Governor John Webster were carried on the shoulders of his fellow townsmen and laid away to rest in the burying-ground, and his loss was deeply felt. His body was committed to the grave by Sexton Richard Montague, who received for the service fifteen shillings.

The Indians still roamed from place to place, begging the planters to plow their fields, and to give them medicines and liquor for fancied ailments. Dr. John Westcarr not only cured their diseases, but sold them "strong water" contrary to law, for which he was fined and admonished. His widow, Hannah, spent his "good estate" for gay silk gowns, for which she was presented in the Northampton court. Hadley people, however, to a good degree, lived a simple life. They ate their dinner when the sun reached the noon mark on the southern window casing, lighted their houses with candle-wood, picked huckleberries in the streets and home lots, feasted on honey stored by wild bees in hollow trees, and washed their garments with soft soap brought from Connecticut by John Pynchon. The hunters shot deer for food and clothing, and waged a relentless warfare upon the wolves which destroyed their flocks. Hogs, with rings in their snouts, and wearing yokes two and one half times the thickness of their necks, ran through Hadley streets. Horses and young cattle grazed on the Pine Plain and along the mountain side.

Thus until 1675 the fifty families which composed the settlement were enabled to maintain themselves, and live in peace and quietness, with none to disagree with them in matters of religious doctrine. They governed their unruly members with a steady hand. The law of the General Court that persons whose estate did not exceed £200 should not wear gold and silver lace, or garments made of silk, was rigorously enforced. The wives of John Westcarr, Joseph Barnard, Thomas Wells, Jr., Edward Granniss, and Joseph Kellogg, and Maiden Mary Broughton, were arraigned before Northampton judges as persons of small estate "wearing silk contrary to law," and were fined, admonished, or acquitted according to the gravity of each offense. Later certain young men were convicted of wearing long hair, and were reprimanded by the court. A fine of three shillings fourpence was imposed "for any person that shall run and race and inordinately Gallopp any Horse in any of Hadley streets."

Parson Russell, in the little square meeting-house on the hill, was the inspiration of the religious life of Hadley, as the building itself was the center of the community. The voice of conscience, interpreted by the voice of the preacher, was more powerful than the weak notes of the bell, and by a life of obedience to its dictates the early settlers hardened themselves against the time of trial which awaited them.

CHAPTER II

A REIGN OF TERROR IN OLD HADLEY

The founders of Hadley were brave and valiant pioneers, ready to fight for their king across the sea, or to defend with their lives their homes and hearthstones. Their pastor, John Russell, was a farmer among farmers, who shared the joys and sorrows of his people. More than this, unknown to his parishioners, the unpretentious country parson was a patriot and a hero. Many years before, when the little plantation was only five years old, there had come, stealing from their New Haven hiding-place, two strangers whom the good minister had received into his home. Political opinions were divided then as now, but Parson Russell hesitated not to protect those whom he believed were persecuted for conscience's sake from their enemies in the new country, who would have delivered them to ignominious death.

These fugitives, members of the High Court of Justice, by which King Charles I of England was dethroned and executed, had, with the restoration of the king's son, Charles II, fled to Boston, where under assumed names they would fain have made

The Meadow Plain and the Holyoke Mountains
Looking Southeast from the River

A Reign of Terror in Old Hadley

their homes. But royal vengeance tarried not. Good friends informed the refugees that officers were on their track, and the hunted men, led by an Indian guide, threaded the forests on foot through Springfield to New Haven, where for a time they were allowed to rest in peace. News that special commissioners for their arrest had arrived in Boston was accompanied by the warning that they were no longer safe on Connecticut soil. Then came the journey by night to Hadley, and the unseen entrance into a dwelling that was indeed to prove a haven of refuge.

Thus beside the simple life of the country minister's home, the unpretentious roof-tree covered a tragedy, for within a secret chamber dwelt the regicide judges, General Edward Whalley and General William Goffe, each with a price upon his head. The children and servants of the household went in and out, and knew not of the strangers' presence. Peter Tilton and other good friends brought letters and supplies sent to Boston from the wife and daughter in Old England, and carried messages in return. In this rural home the cousin of Oliver Cromwell, and his son-in-law, chief officers in the Lord Protector's army, dragged out the remnant of their lives in constant apprehension of discovery. Creeping forth at night, they may have been seen by a belated traveler, but such an one, imagining that spirits walked abroad, disturbed them not. By day, if alarms arose, they descended through the trap-door in their closet to the cellar, and there remained concealed. Deprived of all companionship, with little news from the outside world, their lingering hopes grew fainter, until, it is believed, about 1676, the old man Whalley died, and was buried in an unknown grave. With the safety and maintenance of these fugitives, added to the many other cares upon his mind and heart, the friendly host and jailer settled the petty details of every-day life, adjusted disputes with regard to seating the meeting-house, and looked sharply after the interests of the grammar school, on which depended the educational welfare of the youth.

Suddenly, one morning, when not a cloud was in the sky, the sound of heavy ordnance, as of great guns firing charge after charge, shook the earth, and could not be explained. Frightened by this strange phenomenon, the despised red "salvages," considered to be as harmless as the lazy dogs about the doors, disappeared from their accustomed haunts. The record states: "They plucked up their wigwams and took away the goods they had laid up in our houses."

News of the Indian uprising led by King Philip had reached Hadley, and the strange actions of the natives about the settlement had been noted, but rather with relief than alarm. Wise men were anxious, but the majority felt no fear. Was not the whole county protected by the "Hampshire Troop of Horsemen," under the leadership of Captain John Pynchon of

A Reign of Terror in Old Hadley

Springfield? When this famous company paraded up and down Hadley street, in uniforms decked with gold and silver lace and gay silk sashes, with gaudy trappings for the horses, the Indians looked on in speechless admiration, eager to see the red flag flutter and to hear the martial strains. And, although less than twenty Hadley men were enrolled in this troop, yet did not the Indians know that every farmer had a musket, and a pike fourteen feet long, and that some had also the lighter snaphance, with barrel three and one half feet in length? The Hadley militia also was ready for defense, with Samuel Smith as its lieutenant, and Aaron Cooke, Jr., for its ensign. Civilized men, thus armed and well drilled in the fifty-eight postures of the gun, and the various maneuvers of the pike, ought surely to be able to cope with naked, ignorant savages. Thus reasoned many, when almost without warning a breathless runner brought tidings of the massacre at Brookfield, and terror reigned in every heart.

The Indians in the fort across the river, upon hearing the news, gave "eleven triumphing shouts," waking the echoes far and near. Too late the settlers realized the folly of having so carelessly supplied the natives with guns, and attempted peaceably to disarm them, but in vain. Their headquarters was the Indian fort half-way between Northampton and Hatfield. Captains Lothrop and Beers, with about one hundred men, crossed the river to Hatfield, while reenforcements from Northampton came to meet them, intending to parley with the Indians and to try to persuade them to give up their weapons. They found the fort deserted, but, as they were following the trail, suddenly the enemy, hidden in the woods, "let fly 40 guns." The fight lasted three hours, during which nine men from nine different towns were killed, Azariah Dickinson, son of Nathaniel, of Hadley, being among the first to fall. Too late the soldiers realized that men accustomed to march in bodies, though well trained in the arts of war, could not compete with an unseen foe, concealed behind trees and unencumbered with clothing. Pikes and heavy muskets were of no avail. This was the beginning of sorrows.

Rev. Solomon Stoddard, in his story of these battles, says: "Many sins are so grown in fashion that it becomes a question whether they be sins or not," and especially mentions "intolerable pride in clothes and hair." The Puritans firmly believed that calamities came in punishment for sin. The Hadley people were not able now, however, to spend much time in repentance for minor transgressions, as safety was to be secured only by constant vigilance. At this time, according to an oft-told tale, the settlers were observing a fast day service in the church when it was surrounded and attacked by a body of Indians. "Suddenly, in the midst of the people, there appeared a man of very

A Reign of Terror in Old Hadley

venerable aspect and different from the inhabitants in his apparel, who took the command, arranged and ordered them in the best military manner, and under his direction they repelled and routed the Indians and the town was saved. . . . The inhabitants could not account for the phenomenon, but by considering that person as an Angel of God. . . . The Angel was certainly General Goffe." Thus runs the tale as related by the historian of olden time. For many years this story was believed, and the scene, as depicted in the old engraving, "The Angel of Hadley," is to-day preserved in many homes. Sir Walter Scott, in Peveril of the Peak, related the incident, and only recently has the modern historian discovered that Hadley was not attacked that day, September, 1675, and that the story is based only upon a tradition which has no real foundation.

But though this particular attack may not have been made, yet the air was full of rumors of war, and the panic-stricken inhabitants lived in constant expectation of slaughter and destruction. We can hardly realize the terror of those days in the unprotected hamlet, when the forests all about seemed filled with the shadows of unseen foes. Again and again, alarmed by some unknown cause, the cattle and horses came rushing into the clearing in a wild stampede, and the women and children hid in the darkest corners of their homes, and held their breath for fear. Captain

Lothrop, with seventy men, started toward Deerfield to act as a guard for a train of carts laden with grain for Hadley. A sudden attack at Muddy Brook caused its waters to flow red with the blood of fifty-four soldiers and seventeen teamsters, taken off their guard as they were plucking grapes by the roadside, while the brave captain, attempting to rally his men, fell to rise no more. The words of the historian give but little idea of the desolation which that fated expedition brought to many happy homes. He says: "This was a black and fatal day, wherein were 8 persons made widows and 20 children made fatherless, all in one little plantation, and above 60 persons buried in one dreadful grave." The brook, so muddy then, has since been known as Bloody Brook. The "dreadful grave" is marked by a monument with an appropriate inscription that all the world may read. John Barnard, son of Francis Barnard of Hadley, was among the teamsters slain on this expedition.

Alarmed by this calamity, the Commissioners of the New England Colonies despatched three hundred Massachusetts militia and two hundred Connecticut soldiers for the defense of Hampshire County. Major Pynchon was in Hadley commanding these forces when an express reached him in the middle of the night with the warning that five hundred of King Philip's men were in readiness to fall upon Springfield. Almost frantic the Major with his troops started toward

A Reign of Terror in Old Hadley 29

the south, to see afar off the sky red with the flames of thirty-two blazing houses, only thirteen remaining unharmed. This disaster was not wrought by Philip, but by the near neighbors and sometime friends under Wequogon, that peaceful sachem who signed the deed by which the meadow of Hockanum was added to Hadley. That those who had almost been inmates of their homes could do such fearful wrong to their benefactors created in the hearts of the settlers a desire for revenge. By order of the soldiers an old squaw was torn to pieces by dogs, and other cruel acts unworthy of a civilized people were committed. Good Parson Russell, feeling the helplessness of men, wrote: "Our town of Hadley is now like to drink next, if mercy prevent not, of this bitter cup. We are but about 50 families and now left solitary. We desire to repose our confidence in the living and eternal God who is the refuge of his people."

The winter of 1675 and 1676 was a season of gloom. The Indians seldom fought when the trees were destitute of leaves, and so it was determined to prepare for a state of siege. In spite of the cold and storm all able-bodied men were compelled to work upon the "palisaides," which were built crossing the home lots behind the buildings on both sides of the street, and across at either end. Solid stakes of timber eight feet long were split and sharpened, then driven close together two feet into the ground. To these were nailed heavy horizontal slabs a few inches below the top, thus making a fence too high and formidable to climb and too thick for bullets to penetrate. This fortified enclosure was about a mile long, with strong gates in each of the four sides. The fighting men were divided into military watches, called squadrons, and constant guard was kept both night and day. Rumors were abroad that Philip and his men were hovering near, and though all these reports were unconfirmed, yet in imagination the mountain sides swarmed with the followers of that dreaded chieftain whose very name struck terror to the bravest heart. One morning in April, 1676, Deacon Richard Goodman, with a party of men, went cautiously out to work in Hockanum meadow. The deacon carelessly moved a little beyond the guards, the better to observe his fences, when he fell shot through the heart, and a scouting party, rushing from the woods, seized upon Thomas Reed and dragged him away. Thus a widow and eight children were added to the helpless ones to be maintained and protected by the town fathers. After this it was ordered that when the farmers were haying in Hockanum and Fort meadows all the garrison, except eight left for the security of the women and children, should attend them as a guard, and that not less than forty nor more than fifty men at one time should work in the meadows.

About this time Samuel Smith, Lieutenant of the

"train-band," being near eighty years of age, requested to be freed from military service, and Philip Smith, his son, was chosen in his place. That same year Joseph Kellogg was an ensign, and the next year he was promoted to be lieutenant. Aaron Cooke, who was captain of the militia for thirty-five years, inherited from his father a book entitled "The Compleat Body of the Art Military," and from his study of this probably acquired his excellence in the profession of arms. But the glory of the Hampshire troopers caused the plain militia men to seem but insignificant, although when active service was required the farmer soldiers were always at the front.

The minister's house being the headquarters of the officers of the troop, it has been supposed that Goffe, the regicide, removed to the home of Peter Tilton, where he remained the rest of his life. Others believe that fearing it would be impossible to keep his presence a secret when the town and even his place of refuge was filled with soldiers, Parson Russell contrived to have his guest escorted to Hartford, and settled among friends. The fact that Goffe's diary, from which much is learned about his life in New England, was found among the effects left by Parson Russell, gives us reason to believe that the wanderer was permitted to return and spend his last days in Hadley among the few faithful ones entrusted with the secret of his presence. Communication with his wife and children failed, and for this reason, wherever he was, he died a broken-hearted man. The tradition in Hadley that two strangers were buried in Parson Russell's cellar gives rise to the belief that the graves of both regicides may have been concealed beneath that gloomy chamber where they had so often taken refuge. Wherever their graves may have been, their poor bodies remained undiscovered, and rested in peace.

Thomas Reed, the captive carried away from Hockanum meadow, escaped and returned with the information that the Indians were gathering in force near Deerfield and were "secure and scornful," boasting of great things they had done and should do. Alarmed by this report the troops and citizens of the river towns agreed to strike a decisive blow at the enemy, and if possible to attack him in his camp by night. A company of fifteen Hadley men, under sergeants John Dickinson and Joseph Kellogg, crossed the upper ferry and joined the mounted force of one hundred and fifty soldiers from Springfield, Westfield, Northampton, and Hatfield, commanded by Captain William Turner. The Indian encampment was reached under cover of the darkness, according to the plan, and the inmates suffered a "great and notable slaughter"; but the outcome of the expedition was disastrous, for on the return march the Indians fell upon the line, killed Captain Turner and thirty-eight of his men, and captured others, some of whom were afterward tortured and burned at the stake. Isaac Harrison and John Crow of Hadley were among the victims, and Jonathan Wells, wounded and suffering, reached the settlement after wandering three days in the woods. A great number of Indians perished in this "Falls Fight," and many were drowned in the river. The loss of the English was so great, however, that it could hardly be considered a victory on their part, for the Indian camp was not broken up, and those remaining were aroused to a greater fury by the attack, which resulted in the death of many of their women and children.

It seemed now most imperative that the headquarters of the Indians should be permanently destroyed so that the settlers could cultivate their fields and harvest their crops in peace. With this in view another expedition into Hampshire County was organized by soldiers from Connecticut and southern Massachusetts, and the first division, consisting of two hundred and fifty mounted Englishmen and two hundred friendly Indians on foot, started from Norwich and on the seventh day arrived in Hadley hungry and footsore. The horsemen were mostly from towns along Long Island Sound, and the Indians were Pequots, Mohegans, and Niantics, whose appearance in the streets almost caused a panic, as the inhabitants had never before seen so large a body of friendly Indians together, and could not realize that although they had copper-colored faces, their "hearts were white." June 8, while waiting for the Massachusetts contingent, a great parade was held, and the "Army from Connecticut," four hundred and fifty strong, with colors flying, marched up and down Hadley street to the sound of drum and fife. Provisions of bread, pork, and liquor were brought from Norwich, but not in a sufficient quantity to satisfy the soldiers, who were billeted in the homes of the citizens, and fed with such supplies as could be secured. Their bread was found to be unfit for use on account of a "blue mould" with which it was discolored, and the tobacco demanded was difficult to obtain.

The town was filled with troops and every home was crowded in most uncomfortable fashion. Joseph Kellogg and Samuel Partrigg were kept busy ferrying passengers and horses across the river, Samuel Porter acted as a nurse, Richard Montague, the grave-digger, baked the soldiers' bread, and Timothy Nash repaired their arms. Dr. William Locke, who came to Hadley with Captain Lothrop, dressed wounds and dispensed physic to each in turn, as need required. Mr. Russell recorded that the board of the officers, whom he entertained, was paid, but that his wife Rebecca never received anything for her great "trouble, cumber and care." Probably at this time she was assisted by the negro slaves whom her husband left as part of his estate. Those of the citizens who were inclined to

A Reign of Terror in Old Hadley 35

murmur were thankful indeed when what might have been a terrible calamity was turned into a victory by the presence of their troublesome guests.

June 12, 1676, a double surprise occurred, for about two hundred river Indians, not knowing that four hundred and fifty soldiers from the south had recently arrived, made an attack on Hadley and were "terribly frighted with the report and slaughter made amongst them by the Great Gun." Whether the town had obtained this terrible weapon, or whether the soldiers brought it with them, we cannot tell, and the enemy did not stop to find out. It was only a very small cannon, but it did good service on this and other occasions and caused the Indians to keep at a respectful distance. This attack aroused the settlers to take extra precautions for the safety of the helpless ones entrusted to their care. Stockades were built around the meeting-house that the women and children might have a place of refuge in case the enemy should get inside the fortifications. Every man was compelled to go to meeting armed, or to pay a fine of twelvepence, and his arms were not to be stacked at the door but were to lie ready at his hand. In this manner the Hadley people lived, year after year, fearing for their lives until the very fear became a custom. Armed men gathered in town-meeting and voted to build new fortifications, with rails ten feet long and three inches thick, set two feet into the ground. Each squadron erected a watch house within whose shelter one of their number always was on guard. All the males over sixteen, with an escort of soldiers, went out to clear the Pine Plain east of the town to make it fit for pasture. The Indians burned the corn mill with the house adjoining, and continued their depredations on outlying property which was of necessity left unguarded. It was hoped that the death of King Philip in 1676 might bring the Indian warfare to a close, but his followers, having tasted blood, were no longer dependent on him as a leader in their struggle with the whites. War between England and France caused friction among the colonies, and resulted in battles in which the Indians were used as allies, and many more years of anxiety were spent in "scouting in woods," "watching by day and warding by night," repairing fortifications, and raising the wherewithal to pay the burdensome taxes. Hadley, at this time having three hundred and twelve inhabitants, had a curious way of settling accounts. The town, being indebted to a citizen, subtracted his tax rate and the rates of others to whom he owed money, and paid him the balance in wheat and Indian corn.

Realizing that war was demoralizing, those in authority tried to exercise the greater watchfulness as to the manners of the people. Gershom Hawkes was fined for having in his possession a pack of cards, and refusing to tell where he obtained them, and "Joseph

Kellogg, Jr., and Gershom Hawkes were fined 10s. each for breach of the Sabbath, having travelled till midnight the night before the Sabbath." The genealogy tells us that the said Gershom Hawkes "died young," so his unruly actions did not long trouble his associates, and probably Joseph Kellogg, senior, was not sorry. Jane Jackson, servant of Lieutenant Philip Smith, was given twenty lashes on her bare back before the court for stealing from her master. Parents were obliged to pay for glass in the meeting-house windows broken by their mischievous boys. Samuel Nash, nine years old, having been killed by a fall from his horse, which was frightened by a dog, the boy's father brought suit against Mr. Goodwin, the owner of the dog. The jury returned the following verdict: "It doth not appear yt Mr. Goodwin or Mrs. Goodwin had sufficient notice given them of their dog's curstness or any warning to restrayne their dog, and therefore the Corte doth acquit them, and accounteth Goodman Nash or his wife blameworthy in not having a more strict watch over their son, but letting him goe to fetch ye mare from pasture with such mean tackling."

As if Hadley had not enough to endure from within and without, to the natural fears of her citizens were added superstitious terrors, for in the midst of the second Indian war Mrs. Mary Webster, reputed to be a witch, began to cast an evil eye about her to see what mischief she might do. As a consequence, cattle would stop in front of her house and stand trembling until by her magic power she allowed them to pass. A load of hay, upset by her machinations, returned to its normal position without help from human hands, when the woman was threatened by the driver. She entered the door of a neighbor's house, when lo, the baby in the cradle was raised three feet in air, and replaced by an unseen power upon its pillow. A hen flew down the chimney into a pot of boiling water, and the witch was found to be suffering from a scald. Enraged, the citizens "haled her down to Boston," where, after trial, she was acquitted and returned in triumph to her home, only to revenge herself upon Deacon Philip Smith, "a man for devotion, sanctity, gravity and all that was honest, exceeding exemplary."

This valuable citizen was, according to Cotton Mather, "murdered with an hideous witchcraft." "A wretched woman of the town, being dissatisfied at his just care about her, expressed herself unto him in such a manner that he declared himself apprehensive of receiving mischief at her hands." He began to be "very valetudinarious" and, after wonderful manifestations in the sick-room, died, and his body was found "full of holes that seemed to be made with awls," all of which is related in the Magnalia, with full particulars added. While the sufferer was yet alive, a number of brisk lads dragged the witch out of the house, hung her up until nearly dead, and then buried her in the snow, but, according to the record, "It happened that she survived and the melancholy man died." Mary Webster lived eleven years after her hanging, and died a natural death, a proof to many minds that she really was a witch.

Parson John Russell, after the death of both the regicides had removed the shadow from his home, was able to devote more time and energy to the work among his chosen people. His letters from Hadley to officials in Boston, during the Indian wars, contain much valuable information concerning the history of the town. May, 1665, he preached the election sermon at Boston, taking for his text the words, "Pray for the peace of Jerusalem. They shall prosper that love Thee." This appeal from one living in Hadley at that critical period was most significant and must have come home to every heart. Worn out with Indian alarms, hiding regicides, and fighting witchcraft, on December 10, 1692, John Russell, the first minister of Hadley, died, and in the depth of winter his body was carried to the burying-ground and laid beside his wife Rebecca. The inscription on the table of sandstone placed above his grave is studied to-day with exceeding interest by the many visitors to this historic cemetery. His memory is honored as that of one who was, by virtue of his courage and fidelity, the hero of Old Hadley.

CHAPTER III

THE CHURCH IN OLD HADLEY

I. *The Pastorate of Rev. Isaac Chauncey*

THE bell procured in 1690 by Goodman Partrigg rang out a clamorous peal at early dawn the 16th of October, 1695, and soon the voters of Hadley were wending their way to the little meeting-house on the hill. The forests were resplendent in gay autumnal garb, but the town fathers, intent on business vital to the welfare of the community, had no time to note the beauties of nature. With guns in hand, they took their seats in the dilapidated sanctuary, and there, in town-meeting assembled, voted: "That we doe ernestly desire ye Rev. Mr. Isack Chancy that he would be pleased to settle amongst us to be our minister."

Immediately after Parson Russell's death, two "messengers" had been appointed to secure a pastor, but the candidates discovered, Samuel Moody and Simon Bradstreet, though acceptable in the pulpit, each required as salary more corn, wheat, and peas than the people could afford to pay. At last, July, 1695, Rev. Isaac Chauncey, son of Parson Israel Chauncey of

First Church and Town Hall

The Church in Old Hadley

Stratford, and grandson of Rev. Charles Chauncey, the august president of Harvard College, was engaged as a supply, and the hearts of his hearers were taken by storm. In their cautious and dignified manner they proceeded to make overtures to this bright young preacher, and were rejoiced when he accepted their call, on terms with which they could comply. The parish bought of Samuel, the son of Parson Russell, the home of their first minister for £120, and spent £20 on repairs and improvements. They offered Mr. Chauncey the home lot and buildings, twenty acres of meadow land, a salary of £70 a year in "provision pay," for three years, and afterwards £80 annually and his firewood. After his ordination the new pastor betook himself straightway to some unknown place for Sarah, his bride, and the newly married pair set themselves bravely at work to do their utmost in the parish to which the Lord had called them. The enthusiastic utterance of a youth but twenty-five years old, and fresh from Harvard College, must have caused some agitation among the grave and reverend fathers in his congregation, but their minds were so much perturbed by alarms from without that they had no inclination to quarrel with their minister, who soon was to be called upon for sympathy and consolation in an hour of urgent need.

A party of Indians from Albany, encamped above Hatfield, though supposed to be friendly, were the cause of much anxiety to the elders in the community, who, remembering the days of old, felt their presence to be a menace. Another typical October morning dawned in the lovely valley. Richard Church, the Hadley tailor, and grandson of Richard the first settler, accompanied by Samuel Barnard and Ebenezer Smith, went hunting in the eastern woods. Toward night two badly frightened boys rushed into the broad street, with news that after leaving their companion they had heard gun shots, accompanied by savage yells, away in the depths of the forest. Then there was gathering of forces from three neighboring towns, and hurried departure through the evening shadows, and noiseless searching among rocks and underbrush and fallen trunks of trees, until, almost at daybreak, the seekers found the object of their quest. Transfixed by arrows and mutilated by bullets, with scalp torn away and clothing destroyed, the body of Richard Church was tenderly carried to the home where waited his poor young bride, Sarah Bartlett, and his mother, Widow Mary Church.

Determined that the murderers should be punished, the friends and neighbors of the hapless young man started in hot pursuit, and having had long years of training in the ways of savage warriors, beat the red miscreants at their own game. The guilty Indians were discovered deep hidden in a cave on the west end of Mount Toby, and were "haled" not too gently to Northampton, loaded with irons hastily constructed by the village blacksmith, and, as there was no prison, were confined in a private house with a grim constable as their jailer. John Pynchon, Samuel Partrigg, Joseph Hawley, and Aaron Cooke, "Esquires," and Joseph Parsons, "Gentleman," were especially commissioned to hold a court of Oyer and Terminer, October 21, 1696, for the trial of these cases, and Sheriff Samuel Porter of Hadley took care that the criminals were produced before the judges. Other Indians, frightened at the determination of the settlers, turned state's evidence and the prisoners were speedily convicted and sentenced to be shot to death. Their execution in Northampton was witnessed by an immense crowd from all the country round. This was the first instance of capital punishment in Hampshire County. Thus with a tragedy among his people was inaugurated the pastorate of Rev. Isaac Chauncey, and one of the first duties of that opening year must have been to extend the consolations of religion to the widowed bride and bereaved mother of Richard Church.

Mr. Chauncey came to Hadley just in time to settle the controversy about the dignity of the seats in the meeting-house gallery. It was voted that "Ye first seat in ye front gallerye is look to be eaquall with ye second seat in the body of ye meeting-house, and that ye west end of ye side gallerye to be eaquall with ye third seat in ye body of ye meeting-house." The building itself, having been used as a fort and place of refuge for so many years, was in a dilapidated condition, but war time was not a propitious season in which to build a new one. At last the peace of Utrecht ended the long struggle, and the citizens thanked God and took courage.

Now came a busy time for Hadley. Her people, cooped up so long behind the fortifications, tore down the stockades, planted new fields, mended the fences, repaired their dwellings, and resumed the business of peaceful every-day life. The work of collecting turpentine from pine trees and shipping it to Hartford, though very profitable, had to be restricted lest all the pines remaining be permanently injured. The town gave Deacon Smith and Lieutenant Nash permission to get turpentine from the trees on Spruce Hill, the quantity not to exceed one thousand boxes. The turpentine was often exchanged for rum, as minister and deacons and all the church members drank liquor as regularly as they ate their daily bread, and the licensed innkeepers, Hezekiah Dickinson and Joseph Smith, could not buy or make enough to supply their guests. Sometimes men were allowed to sell rum in their own homes, as in the case of Richard Goodman, who was a "retailer" before he kept the ferry. Philip Smith was permitted to sell to those "in real need," and Samuel Partrigg to sell to the "neighbors." Andrew Warner was a "Maltster," and Samuel Porter had a "still and worm," and doubtless both ministered to these "real needs" of neighbors far and near. Orange Warner was the last maltster of Hadley. But altogether the people could not manufacture enough of any kind of drink to satisfy the demand, so aqua vitæ was imported, and rum was brought in hogsheads and sold in small amounts to those inveterate drinkers, who seldom became drunken.

Visitors to the valley, after its people had repaired the ruin wrought by the Indian wars, saw perched upon Hadley hill a fine new meeting-house, modern in style as became the temple in which a progressive people worshiped the Lord. The little old first edifice was falling in pieces when, in 1713, another important town-meeting was held, over which Samuel Porter presided as moderator. Here the people voted "That we will build a new Metting Hous" and "That the Meting house that we have agreed to build shall be 40 foot in length and 40 foot in breadth, with a flattish roof and a Bellcony on one end of said house." The committee, Samuel Porter, "Left." Nehemiah Dickinson, "Sargt." Daniel Marsh, Peter Montague, and Samuel Barnard, were instructed to buy glass, nails, "clabbords," and shingles, and to hire workmen, "improving our own inhabitants as conveniently as may be."

The second meeting-house was finished in 1714, and stood for ninety-five years. The "flattish roof" would now be considered steep. The "bellcony," built up from the ground, was the first steeple in Hampshire County. The bell tower was probably not at once completed, the committee finding it necessary to get the frame raised and covered and plastered, and to set the "joyners" windows firmly in their places, before spending time and money on what was purely ornamental. The beams overhead were hidden by plastering, but the posts and braces were painted and left in sight. When the building was almost finished "Captain Aaron Cooke, Esq., Ensign Chileab Smith, Mr. Samuel Porter, Esq., Jonathan Marsh, Deac. Nathaniel White and Deac. John Smith" put their wise heads together in a vain endeavor to seat the new meeting-house in a manner more acceptable to the aristocracy than had been the arrangement in the old one. In 1717 more pews were built, the gallery and desk were painted, "pentices" were placed over the doors, and efforts were made to keep the rain from spoiling the plastering by beating under the eaves. After a time Eleazer Porter, son of Samuel, the first settler, replaced the simple pulpit and sounding-board with new ones more elegant than those in Northampton or Hatfield, and also presented a handsome new desk for the minister's use. The children gazed with wonder on the elaborate wooden canopy which seemed to project in air with no visible support above the parson's head, and threatened to come down with a crash when in tremendous tones the reverend speaker thundered forth the terrors of the law. Their fears were not without reason, for, although through all these theological thunderings the sounding-board remained firm, yet the little diamond-shaped panes of glass did become loosened from the leads which held them and were replaced in a firmer fashion with "square glass" of a later style. Square pews built by individuals, and considered much more respectable than narrow slips, took the place of the old-fashioned long seats. Eleazer Porter owned a square pew, and other well-to-do people built similar ones, with supports fastened to the floor, so there could be no clattering, such as was heard in many churches when children moved about.

Seating the meeting-house continued to produce hot contentions, as the selectmen were obliged to regard "age, estate," and many sorts of "qualifications." Heads of families sat in their pews in the body of the house, and females in the gallery on the right, while the males were on the left. After 1772 the front seats in the side galleries were reserved for singers. Little children on low benches in the aisles were ever conscious of the keen old eyes watching them from the gallery where the tithing man was on the lookout for offenders. At any appearance of levity, with a sharp rap on the top of the seat his official staff would be pointed directly at the unlucky wight, who, conscious of the reproving gaze of the whole congregation, wished that the floor might open and swallow him up. Before the pulpit, opposite the broad aisle, sat the deacons in a solemn row. On the top of the partition next the aisle was balanced the christening basin, and here the minister performed the rite of baptism, often on infants but twenty-four hours old. A leaf which hung near by, when raised, was covered with a white cloth, and upon the table thus made were placed the bread and wine for the communion service. Among the communicants in an upper region were certain chattels with black faces, the property of their brethren in the Lord.

We should imagine that those old Puritan fathers would have regarded with scorn any attempt to enslave a weaker race, as contrary to those principles on which their very faith was founded. But our heroic ancestors were human and therefore inconsistent. They always had an eye for business ventures which promised gain, and settled the matter with their consciences as best they could. For more than one hundred years slavery existed in the valley towns and the masters and mistresses were among the most respected of their citizens. Joshua Boston, chattel, a consistent member of the Hadley church, with dignified carriage and gentlemanly manners, was an important member of the family of Eleazer Porter. His ability to read and write enabled him to become well posted in the news of the day, so that, although a slave, he was glad to fight for the cause of liberty in the Revolution. We may well believe that at his death his master felt that he had lost property worth £20, at which old Joshua was valued. Joshua's funeral was attended by many friends, who mourned him for his worth, irrespective of the color of his skin. During a period of six years thirteen negroes died in Hadley and were buried in the old cemetery. The funerals of these servants were "improved" by the ministers as occasions upon which it was proper to defend the institution of slavery and endeavor to reconcile the slave to his bonds. Whipping was the customary punishment for common offenses, yet in those days when stocks and whipping-post and ducking-stool were in active operation for white criminals, this penalty may not have been excessive. The Hadley slaves were treated much like children, and were not subjected to more severe discipline than were the sons and daughters of their owners.

Parson Isaac Chauncey was a conscientious man. He preached long sermons in which were clearly portrayed the principles of right and justice, yet, like his predecessor, he was a slaveholder and saw no harm in following a practice which he believed was taught in the Old Testament scriptures. His helpmeet, Sarah, died when thirty-eight years old, leaving ten children. The father of this family was also the master of Arthur Prutt, Joan, his wife, and their dusky brood of seven, named respectively, George, Elenor, Ishmael, Cæsar, Abner, Zebulon, and Chloe.

The fact that Arthur had a surname indicates that he may have been bought from another rather than imported directly from the African coast. It must have been difficult for the minister to fill so many hungry mouths on the pittance paid for his services, and a Southern planter would have sold some of these young darkies, but we find no proof that this was ever done. It is very probable that each of the parson's daughters, Mrs. John Graham, of Southbury, Conn., Mrs. Grindal Rawson, of South Hadley, Mrs. Daniel Russell, of Rocky Hill, Conn., and Mrs. Hobart Estabrook, of East Haddam, received a slave when she was married to the minister of her choice, and thus the negro family was kept within bounds. George, the son of Arthur Prutt, died in Whately. The parson's son, Richard Chauncey, brought a slave to the East Precinct, afterwards Amherst, and Josiah Chauncey, a prominent resident of the same town, was the master of Cæsar Prutt.

The Chauncey brothers were violent Tories, and Cæsar, the slave, not sympathizing with their sentiments, must have run away, for when Captain Reuben Dickinson raised his famous company at the time of the Lexington alarm, the bondman Cæsar stood side by side with other Amherst residents, and did his duty with the rest. The patriotic slave of a Tory master, knowing the bitterness of servitude, was eager to fight for freedom. Years passed. Josiah Chauncey and his wife left Amherst, and died in Schenectady, New York. The Revolutionary veterans were awarded pensions, but nothing is heard of Cæsar Prutt. At last, when in April, 1801, Amherst held its annual town-meeting in the old church on the hill, the clerk recorded the following: "Voted, that Cæsar Prutt, a Town Pauper, be Set up at Vendue to the lowest bidder for Vitualling and Beding, and was Struck off to Asa Smith for one year for One Dollar Per week." Alas for Cæsar! We can imagine the decrepit old Revolutionary hero, with black face and snowy wool and trembling, knotted hands, standing before his fellow townsmen, as they auction him off for one dollar per week. Asa Smith, tired of his undertaking, passed his charge along to Samuel Hastings, and thus the sorry tale goes on. Each year, more feeble and infirm, old Cæsar is brought to the town-meeting and sold to the lowest bidder. Suddenly, in 1806, the record ends, and probably the life went out as a candle is extinguished, leaving but little trace behind. In some unknown corner of West Cemetery in Amherst the wornout body was laid away, and his very name was forgotten.

The name of Zebulon, the youngest son of Arthur Prutt, will forever be connected with the history of the ancient bird that perches on the Hadley meeting-house steeple. When the belfry, rising almost one hundred feet in air, with pillars and fretwork, was complete, the weather-cock, which for more than one hundred and fifty years has creaked round and round above the broad street, was placed in its lofty position. This glittering fowl, brought over from England, and almost as large as a sheep, was so attractive to the young darky, Zeb Prutt, that he climbed the spire and sitting on the rooster's back crowed in a manner worthy of the biped he bestrode. The gay and frisky Zeb, who seemed to be not cast down by the fact of his servitude, afterward became the property of Oliver Warner of Amherst.

During the pastorate of Parson Chauncey the people of Hadley discovered that the great useless mountain in their midst might be of some practical value. Therefore the town voted to fence in the north side of "Mount holioke" for a cow and sheep pasture. One tenth of the old township of Hadley was, in their opinion, wasted in this mountain, which was simply an obstacle in their way. The Indians had taken refuge in its thickets, cattle had fallen over its precipices, and altogether it was an undesirable possession, separating the citizens from their children who had persisted in leaving the old home for the untried lands beyond. In 1727 twenty-one of the southern settlers, because they were "8 miles from the place of public worship and the way was mountainous and bad," petitioned to be made into a precinct, now South Hadley. Thus the Hadley church gained a second daughter, but lost some valuable supporters. Very soon the "East Inhabitants beyond the Pine Plain" demanded that they also should be "set off," and soon the East Precinct, afterwards Amherst, in its own meeting-house was listening to long sermons by the Rev. David Parsons.

Parson Chauncey, although concealing no regicides within his home, had still an ever present grief in the misfortune which had befallen his dearly beloved eldest son Israel. This brilliant young theologue, a graduate of Harvard in the class of 1724, after teaching in the academy at Hadley, and preaching in Northampton and Housatonic, was sought by the church in Norwalk, Conn., for its vacant pulpit. Suddenly his career was cut short by an attack of violent dementia, brought on by excessive study. With no asylum for a refuge, the "distracted young man" was confined in a small outhouse in his father's yard, and his midnight shriekings of "fire" passed unnoticed as the ravings of a maniac. Alas, there came a night when the alarm was all too true, and the poor lunatic cried in vain until his room was wrapped in flames which were discovered too late to save his life.

Before the death of his son the Hadley minister had been in great demand for services outside the town. In Sunderland, at the ordination of Rev. William Rand, and at the funeral of Rev. John Williams of Deerfield, he spoke acceptable words of counsel and sympathy, and when the Rev. Robert Breck of Springfield, pronounced to be a heretic by one company of Hampshire County ministers, was finally admitted by a second and more liberal council, Mr. Chauncey preached the ordination sermon and gave the charge. The tragedy in his home brought on physical ailments which made it necessary for him to have assistance in the pulpit, and he preached but little after 1738, although he lived until 1745. October 16, 1740, George Whitefield, the English evangelist, who by the sober citizens of Hatfield was refused admission to their pulpit, preached in the Hadley meeting-house and, waxing fervent in his speech, thundered so loud that his voice was heard across the river.

II. *The Pastorates of Rev. Chester Williams and Dr. Samuel Hopkins*

Rev. Chester Williams was ordained pastor in Hadley, January 21, 1741, and when good Parson Chauncey passed peacefully to his reward, his brisk young colleague, already in the harness, took full charge of pulpit and parish. This new minister, the son of Rev. Ebenezer Williams of Pomfret, Conn., was graduated at Yale in 1735, and soon after his settlement married Sarah, the daughter of Hon. Eleazer Porter, a wealthy and influential citizen of Hadley. The village, no longer a fortified town, was now a thriving rural hamlet. The twenty-one highways, laid out in

1722 by Samuel and Experience Porter and Lieutenant John Smith, had been improved and widened, and cleared from stones and stumps. Joseph Kellogg, a son of Lieutenant Joseph, kept the ferry at the Aqua Vitæ Meadow. Westwood and Noah Cooke, Ichabod Smith, Joseph Hubbard, Samuel Dickinson, James Goodman, Ezekiel Kellogg, and Benjamin Church, all grandsons of the first settlers, dwelt either in the old homesteads or had built houses for themselves on the broad street. The Marsh family was represented by the aged brothers, Ebenezer and Job, grandsons of John, the pioneer, and their descendants. Captain Job Marsh had built in 1715 a house on land given by the town to his father, Daniel, which is the site of the present meeting-house and town hall. Valiant Captain Moses Marsh, his son, fought in the Louisburg campaign, and after the war settled in his native town and became a most useful and public-spirited citizen. Moses Cooke, the son of Aaron, and possibly others of his generation, were in 1745 still living, and could relate stirring tales of their youthful days when Hadley was besieged like a citadel of old. For the most part the town was a settlement of farmers, and fighting was a well-nigh forgotten art. Lieutenant Noah Cooke was making rope from hemp raised on his land, and Oliver Warner, the hatter, was supplying his neighbors with headgear of the latest style. Some articles of luxury had been introduced, and the aristocrats were carrying gold and silver watches, and warming their feet by means of wooden stoves lined with tin made by Eliakim Smith and Samuel Gaylord. Moses Porter had imported a "chair" in which he drove about, and Parson Williams, dressed in the height of fashion, was a conspicuous figure as, mounted on the most valuable saddle horse in the county, he rode up and down the street making his pastoral calls. His wardrobe included one cloak, one gown, two greatcoats, six coats, six waistcoats, five pairs of breeches, seven shirts, six neckcloths, three cotton handkerchiefs, three bands, five stocks, seventeen pairs of stockings, and smaller articles too many to enumerate. Silver shoe, knee, and stock buckles, gold sleeve buttons and rings, a silver tankard and snuffbox, were also numbered among his possessions. When we realize that nine years of married life brought to his home six children we do not wonder that Phillis, a negro slave, was needed in the parson's kitchen.

At this time Jonathan Edwards was preaching in Northampton and all the churches were involved in the controversy regarding the necessary qualifications for communion. A majority of the ministers in the county disagreed with Mr. Edwards' teaching that the Lord's supper was not a converting ordinance. Rev. Chester Williams, the Hadley minister, was the scribe of that memorable council, by which the greatest preacher of New England was sent away in disgrace, and Parson Williams, together with Enos Nash, the Hadley delegate, voted for his dismission. Three years after this occurred Mr. Williams was seized with a sudden and fatal illness, and again the Hadley church was without a pastor.

Some mysterious attraction about this time drew the attention of a young Yale graduate toward Hadley. He was the nephew of Jonathan Edwards, and no doubt had often in his visits to the broad street crossed the river and viewed the pleasant meadows near at hand. But something beside scenery must have caused him to become a "probationer" in the Hadley pulpit. After preaching for six Sabbaths he accepted the church's loud and urgent call to settle in the parish. A special fast-day was appointed to prepare for the ordination, and then, February 26, 1755, the ceremony took place and Rev. Samuel Hopkins became the fourth minister of Hadley. His father, Rev. Samuel Hopkins of West Springfield, preached the sermon, and Rev. Stephen Williams of Longmeadow gave the charge. From church to parsonage was only a short journey, and it seemed supremely fitting that the new minister in caring for his flock should pay especial attention to the family of his predecessor. The sudden attraction for Hadley may be explained by the fact that, as soon as decorum would allow, Rev. Samuel Hopkins married Mrs. Sarah Williams, widow of the late pastor, and thus at twenty-six became the step-father of six small children, the possessor of many changes of raiment, the owner of a handsome library, and the master of a comfortable and well appointed home.

According to the diary kept by Madam Porter, the mother of Mrs. Hopkins, this year, November 18, 1755, "an awful earthquake" shook the ground beneath their feet and alarmed the inhabitants of the whole county, to whom such a phenomenon presaged disaster. But no immediate effects were felt, for although other Hampshire towns had suffered from Indian depredations, yet, since the treaty of Utrecht, Hadley had been unmolested. Encouraged by continued peace, the people had ventured to settle in the outskirts of the town. Two miles to the north, in a sheltered intervale known as Forty Acre Meadow, Moses Porter, great-grandson of Samuel, the first settler, had built in 1752 a commodious dwelling, and installed therein his bride, Mistress Elizabeth Pitkin, granddaughter of Phebe, the third wife of Parson Russell. Hardly had the master of this home welcomed the new minister within its hospitable portals, when military duty called Captain Porter to take command of his company and march to Albany, there to join the regiment of Colonel Williams in its ill-fated expedition against Crown Point on Lake Champlain. Enos Smith, a small Hadley lad, noted with wondering eyes the gorgeous uniform of the sad-faced soldier, who, obeying duty's call, left his heart behind with his unprotected wife and little daughter Elizabeth in the pleasant home which he was to see no more. Far away from all neighbors, Mistress Porter looked well after her household, and kept a brave heart through the long and lonely summer. At last the swift express from the north reached Hadley, and her dread was turned to certain knowledge when she learned that six days before, September 8, her brave husband had fallen in the battle of Lake George, and that his body, stripped of its martial trappings, had been left to the mercy of his foes, only his sword being secured for his family. All Hadley mourned for the intrepid captain and sympathized with his widow, left alone to care for her young daughter and to manage her large estate.

But trials had to be endured in those old days, and Hadley women were too busy to indulge in nervous prostration. Madam Porter with sorrowful face went about her daily tasks, and for forty years was faithful to her husband's memory. Her little Elizabeth, May 13, 1770, was "published" to Mr. Charles Phelps, a young Northampton lawyer, and June 14 the wedding took place. Her son-in-law relieved Madam Porter of her many cares, built the gambrel roof above the old house as we see it to-day, and added to the farm until it included six hundred acres. His daughter, the third Elizabeth, married Rev. Dan Huntington, and his grandson, Frederic Dan, was the late beloved Bishop of Central New York. Madam Porter lived to be seventy-eight years old. Her body was carried from her old home to the riverside, placed in a boat, taken down the stream, and buried in the cemetery beside the headstone which stands as a memorial to her husband, Captain Moses Porter, a hero of Old Hadley.

Rev. Samuel Hopkins, the minister in Hadley during all the years of Madam Porter's widowhood, stands out from history's page a unique and interesting personality, quite different from the typical New England parson of the olden time. We see him in his home, expending his salary of two hundred and twenty-two dollars so prudently that his nine children and six step-children were fed and clothed, strangers were entertained, and a little was laid by for time of need. We follow him as, attired in long-tailed coat, knee breeches, a vest with skirts, and buckled shoes, he calls from house to house, and seated in the chimney corner puffs upon the pipe kept for his use, and makes himself at home. But the listener, waiting to hear the good divine expound the doctrine and the law, is sometimes disappointed when unseemly levity takes the place of improving conversation, for the worthy parson dearly loves a joke, even when the laugh is turned upon himself.

One Sabbath, when dining with Governor Strong, he declined some pudding between services, saying that pudding before preaching made him dull, at which the Governor slyly queried, "Did you not eat pudding for breakfast?" Parson Hopkins asked an invalid if she would not like to have him "preach a lecture" by her bedside, and received the reply that she would indeed, as she had slept but poorly the night before, and his discourses were always soothing. Complaining that a certain man brought him "soft wood," he was told that he did so because the people were given "soft preaching."

But though a joker for six days in the week, on Sunday Parson Hopkins was dignified in manner and of slow delivery, with so much of judicial argument and wisdom in his utterance that an eminent lawyer remarked that he would make a good judge. He often adapted his sermons to the discussion of special events. The "awful earthquake" called forth two discourses, and a cheerful New Year's sermon, January 1, 1764, declared, "This year thou shalt die." His five sons-in-law, Rev. Samuel Spring, Rev. Samuel Austin, Rev. William Riddel, Rev. Leonard Worcester, and Rev. Nathaniel Emmons, often visited Hadley, and preached in the old church, and sometimes the Hadley pastor exchanged with Mr. Hooker of Northampton, and with Mr. Parsons of Amherst.

When the parson, his wife, her aged mother, and twelve children were crowded beneath the ministerial roof-tree, a sudden misfortune befell the household. The winds, howling over the western hills and sweeping across the Hadley meadows, blew a tiny flicker into flame, and at one o'clock in the morning, March 21, 1766, a blaze shot into air which illuminated the country for miles around. Regardless of sermons or silver, the parson hustled his children half naked through the windows, and rushing after them with his little two-weeks-old Polly hugged close to his breast, assured himself that all were safe, and then exclaimed to the raging flames, "Now burn and welcome!" Fortunately Madam Porter saved her almanac, and in it recorded these facts for our information. She also tells us that in eleven days a new frame was raised, and that on November 24 the family moved into the rebuilt dwelling.

The years of Dr. Hopkins' ministry were crowded with events upon which hung the fate of the nation. The Hadley farmers were all ready for revolution, for they had been greatly exasperated by the King's surveyors who confiscated all trees twenty-four inches in diameter a foot above the ground, to be made into masts for the British navy. In 1765 Josiah Pierce recorded in his almanac, "A mob in Hadley on account of logs." The perpetual wrangling over seating the meeting-house was hushed by the call of the minute men to arms. Giles Crouch Kellogg, Phineas Lyman, Oliver Smith, Josiah Pierce, and Jonathan Warner were appointed a committee of correspondence, and later Ebenezer and Moses Marsh, John Cowls, Benjamin Colt, Eliakim Smith, Edmund Hubbard, Warham Smith, and Noah Cooke were added to this committee. In 1774 Josiah Pierce was sent as Hadley's delegate to the first Provincial Congress. A powder house eight feet square was built in the middle lane and in it was stored four and a half barrels of powder. Noah Smith and Warham Smith were sent to Williamstown to get the "great gun that used to belong to the town." On April 29, 1775, at nine o'clock in the morning, news of the battle of Lexington reached Hadley, and at one o'clock fifty volunteers started toward Boston. A committee was appointed to make saltpetre, and Moses Marsh "took the saltpetre oath."

Hon. Samuel Porter, son of Samuel the first settler, and a very wealthy man, died in 1722 leaving an estate of ten thousand dollars. His grandson, Hon. Eleazer Porter, justice of the peace and judge of probate, and Elisha Porter, sheriff of Hampshire County, lived during the Revolution in handsome houses side by side, built probably by their grandfather on land granted to their great-grandfather by the town. They were the sons of Eleazer, who married Sarah Pitkin and died when fifty-nine years old.

The Hon. Eleazer Porter married for his second wife, Susanna, daughter of Rev. Jonathan Edwards. Her word, handed down through her descendants, proves the house in which she lived to have been built in 1713, and therefore that it is the oldest house in town. The visitor to-day gazes with interest on the quaint exterior with projecting second story, examines the handsome scroll over the double front door, and then walks into the narrow hall and up the winding stairs, where low but sunny chambers open out on either hand, and a steep staircase leads to a dark and dismal attic. There we see hewn timbers, some of which were taken from the old house built by Samuel Porter, the first settler, and thus a portion of this ancient mansion dates back to those old days when the town was born. Below, at the right of the narrow hall, and lighted by three windows, with deep window seats, and paneled woodwork, and fireplace six feet wide, and handsome corner cupboard, is the room formerly used as a court room. Across the hall is another apartment of the same size, and in each ceiling massive roof-trees a foot square give ample support to the floor above. After the Hon. Eleazer Porter died, this house was the home of his son, Jonathan Edwards Porter, and others of his race and name have followed until in later years it passed out of the family.

Colonel Elisha Porter, the proprietor of the other Porter house, which was built one year later, received orders January, 1776, to proceed with his regiment to Quebec. Such a journey in the depth of winter required much courage, but was accomplished safely, and the Colonel returned in time to witness the surrender of Burgoyne at the battle of Saratoga, and to make the acquaintance of that hapless officer and gentleman. Colonel Porter then found it necessary to come home to attend to his duties as high sheriff. Soon there was business at Joseph Kellogg's ferry, where a straggling army of Hessian mercenaries, prisoners of war, waited to be set over the river. Hungry and weary, the rank and file of Burgoyne's army were thankful to rest beside the stream, and Colonel Porter, moved by sympathy for the defeated general, well-nigh helpless with illness, extended to him the hospitality of his own home, and allowed his bodyguard to encamp within the dooryard. The round eyes of the six Porter children stared with astonishment at the gay uniforms and gorgeous trappings brought so suddenly to their very door, and Puritanical ears were horrified at the careless speech of those disgusted British soldiers.

The English general found the quiet Hadley home a very haven of rest, and his natural foes converted into kindly hosts, by whose ministrations his strength was restored, and he was able to resume his journey. In taking leave, Burgoyne presented to Colonel Porter the dress sword which he had surrendered and received again at Saratoga. This invaluable relic was left by its owner to his son Samuel and from him descended to his daughter Pamela, who married Dudley Smith. Their son Samuel Smith, and daughter, Miss Lucy Smith, now own the sword of Burgoyne, a three-edged rapier, with embossed silver handle and filigreed guard. The visitor examining the sword is interested to decipher on the blade near the handle the monogram G. R., while on the other side appears the coat of arms with the motto, "Honi soit qui mal y pense." The owners of the sword live in a house built on the site of the old dwelling, which was moved to the rear, where a part of it is still standing.

This passing of Burgoyne through Hadley was the only occasion during the war when the British were in the Connecticut Valley. Hadley soldiers were always in the field, and during their absence the town cared for their families. Large bounties were offered to volunteers, and horses, blankets, and clothing were, through many sacrifices on the part of the citizens, provided for their use. It was even necessary to "sell the Great Gun at vendue" to raise money to help carry on the war. No complete list has been preserved of those who represented Hadley in the Revolution, but we know that Captain Oliver Smith, Captain Moses Marsh, Nehemiah Gaylord, and his son Nehemiah, Josiah Nash, Daniel Bartlett, Ebenezer Pomeroy, Jr., Seymour Kelsey, Francis Traynor, Ichabod Nye, Medad Noble, and Timothy Smith were in active service. In the midst of the war Hadley was threatened with an epidemic of smallpox brought by soldiers returning from the northern campaign. Much prejudice was felt by the ignorant against inoculation,

The Church in Old Hadley

but finally it was decided that it was a necessary measure, and one Sunday morning fifteen patients submitted to the operation in the home of Moses Marsh, to the great scandal of many who felt that by so doing the Sabbath was needlessly broken.

The meeting-house had been reshingled, the bell recast and made heavier, and general repairs completed, when peaceful Hadley was invaded by another army, pursuing Daniel Shays and his adherents of rebellion fame. The snow was piled in drifts, and the roads almost impassable, when General Lincoln and his three thousand soldiers made their camp one memorable Sunday morning, January 13, 1787, on the broad street. Cannon were stationed north of the meeting-house, and preparations were made by which to keep the Sabbath after the good old fashion. Dr. Hopkins being in feeble health, a messenger was sent to Hatfield for Dr. Lyman, and there behind a pulpit built of snow, with the three thousand soldiers as his congregation, the eloquent divine exhorted, preached, and prayed. The shades of the regicides who lived and died in Parson Russell's house across the way may well have graced with their unseen presence this unique Sunday service.

And now, with all rebellions quelled, the time for a new meeting-house seemed to be at hand. Lieutenant Enos Smith, General Samuel Porter, Charles Phelps, Nathaniel White, Captain Daniel White, Captain Elisha

Dickinson, Lieutenant Caleb Smith, Israel Lyman, Josiah Nash, Major Moses Porter, Lemuel Warren, Windsor Smith, and Percy Smith were chosen a general committee. Plans were selected, and November 3, 1806, it was voted that a meeting-house should be built near the site of the old one at the cost of seven thousand dollars, the money to be raised by selling pews, and by a rate upon the town. November 17 a majority of three decided to build the meeting-house on the Back Street. The vote was then reconsidered and referred to an "indifferent committee." Charles Phelps, Samuel Porter, Caleb Smith, and Captain Elisha Dickinson were placed in charge of the finances of the undertaking.

One thing the people had determined, and that was that there should be no room under the new meeting-house for geese, or sheep, or mischievous boys. The Hadley geese had multiplied until almost every family owned a flock, and these ran the streets, huddling at night in front of their owners' houses, and on sunny days crowding under the meeting-house and making such a racket that the effect of the most eloquent preaching was entirely destroyed. The building committee, Charles Phelps, Lieutenant Caleb Smith, and General Samuel Porter, was doubtless instructed as to this point and obeyed orders.

The final vote that the meeting-house should stand near the old one, and that it should be placed east and west, with the steeple at the east, prevailed, and the committee proceeded with its task. Two years later, in 1808, the edifice standing to-day was completed, and on its spire was mounted the historic weather-cock, now freshened and made smart by a new coat of gilding. The old building was sold and moved away, and November 8, 1808, the new meeting-house was dedicated. A new bell was bought at the cost of two hundred dollars. The pews were sold, parts of the north gallery being reserved by the town for the use of males, and parts of the south for females. "Black males" were allowed to sit in the "north arched pew" and "Black females" in the "south arched pew." No hats were to be hung in the building, and stringent rules for behavior were made and posted by the selectmen. The cost of the meeting-house was $8,413 and the sale of seventy-eight pews brought in $7,031. Colonel Elijah Dickinson, Major Moses Porter, and Captain John Hopkins were appointed to borrow on the credit of the town enough money to complete the payment for the building.

III. *Rev. John Woodbridge and His Successors*

Rev. Samuel Hopkins, now aged and infirm, was no longer able to write and deliver those long and learned sermons, so the committee requested him to relinquish a part of his salary, and in 1810 engaged Rev. John Woodbridge for $500 a year as long as Dr. Hopkins lived, together with fifteen cords of wood while he remained single, and thirty cords after he should marry. But the venerable pastor's work was almost done, and soon a great company from all the country round assembled in the meeting-house to pay the last tribute of respect to his memory. Dr. Joseph Lyman preached his funeral sermon, and his people escorted his body to the grave. Four ministers, Lyman of Hatfield, Wells of Whately, Williams of Northampton, and Parsons of Amherst, with Governor Strong and Deacon Ebenezer Hunt of Northampton, acted as pallbearers. Thus they buried Rev. Samuel Hopkins, minister in Hadley for fifty-seven years.

President Timothy Dwight of New Haven inspected the new meeting-house soon after its completion, and described it as a "handsome structure, superior to any other in this country." There in the middle of the broad street, on the historic site occupied by its predecessor, this stately building stood during the years following, while imperceptibly the center of population moved toward the east. The west street people did not care to go so far to church, and so as in olden time "dissensions arose" which in 1840 culminated in removing the meeting-house bodily and placing it in its present location. The solid structure, evidently built after a more substantial fashion than its predecessor, showed no signs of spreading when raised from its foundations, but traveled along in a dignified fashion, and when it reached its destination settled itself to stay.

But though the meeting-house stood firm, many representatives of the old settlers were in a state of turmoil and excitement, and felt that they could not worship God in the new location. The shades of Parson Russell and his old-time congregation cried out in very protest, and would not be appeased. April 1, 1841, Jacob Smith and ninety others asked to be dismissed that they might form another church. Then came a time of councils and discussions and disagreements and disputes. The perplexed ministers, convened in a private house, suggested that the seceders be allowed to worship by themselves for a time, with the hope of reconciliation. President Humphrey of Amherst College went over to see what he could do, and advised that the disgruntled persons be dismissed, which was accordingly done. Then with the help of an ex-parte council these modern "withdrawers" organized, July 15, 1841, at 2 p. m., the Russell church in Hadley, its members being eighteen men and forty-one women, dismissed by the First church as in good standing, and thirty-one others "being in good standing last June." The Russell meeting-house was erected on West Street, and its pews, built by individuals, are to-day the property of the descendants, so that the building cannot be sold, though it has long been closed for church purposes. We find Mr. Woodbridge, having left the First church, preaching in the Russell church, and when the First church wanted Rev. Benjamin Martin for its minister, the council, of which Mr. Woodbridge was a member, refused to ordain him, because he was not orthodox. Another council was called, with Mr. Woodbridge omitted, and then the candidate was received. September 15, 1841, Rev. Warren H. Beaman was settled over the new church in North Hadley, the last child of the mother church, and then just ten years old.

Mr. Woodbridge was succeeded by Rev. John Brown, and he in turn by Rev. Francis Danforth, during whose ministry the meeting-house was moved. Then came Rev. Benjamin Martin, and after him Rev. Roland Ayres, who was installed in the old church January 11, 1848, where he was the faithful and efficient pastor for thirty-six years. In an anniversary sermon he states that in 1873 less than one hundred households were represented in the parish, with sixteen foreign families in the school district. To-day, in the same community, the foreign-born residents and their children form a large part of the population.

Yet still the old church holds its own. Rev. J. S. Bayne preached in its pulpit after Dr. Ayres, and later Rev. E. E. Keedy was in charge. Its present pastor, Rev. Thomas A. Emerson, a graduate of Yale and a newcomer to the valley, recognizes the value of its history and tradition, and the duty of perpetuating the memory of its founders. A band of patriotic women have formed themselves into the Old Hadley Chapter, Daughters of the American Revolution, with the avowed purpose of awakening and fostering an interest in the history of the town.

In 1909 the children of Old Hadley, returning to celebrate its two hundred and fiftieth anniversary, will visit its historic sanctuary. They will find it still on a firm foundation, undisturbed by the clang of trolley or whizz of automobile beneath its very shadow, holding its lofty steeple high above the new church of St. John across the way. The weather-cock creaks proudly round and round as in the days of old, above the airy fretwork of a spire famous for its beauty of construction and delicacy of finish. Mother of many churches round about, this old church is beloved of her children, who rejoice to tell the story of the time-honored edifice, and reverence the memory of the founders of the valley town, who, with strenuous toil, built that first little meeting-house on the hill.

CHAPTER IV

HOPKINS GRAMMAR SCHOOL AND ACADEMY

The founders of Hadley were imbued with a love of learning second only to their reverence for their minister and meeting-house. Education in those old days meant a knowledge of Latin and Greek, and the object of education was to preach the word of God. Girls could not preach and therefore much schooling for them was not deemed needful, but every boy must go to school or his father would be brought up before the magistrate and punished for neglect of duty. Laws to this effect, made by the General Court, were enforced by the selectmen of each town, who, should the parent prove obdurate, were authorized to take the child from his home and place him with a suitable guardian. Heads of families were obliged to catechise their children, to bring them up to a useful trade, to see that they were not out late at night, and to watch lest boys and girls should "talk too much together." The selectmen were ordered to make a list of all the children between six and twelve years old, and to divide the town into districts so that not one truant should escape their notice.

Hopkins School Building. Erected in 1894

In 1647 a law was enacted by which every town of one hundred families was obliged to support a classical grammar school, where children should be fitted for college. These schools, although not free like the school in Boston, were yet a grievous burden to the smaller towns, which, after the minister had been provided for, found nothing left wherewith to pay a schoolmaster. Parents all desired that the children should learn to read and to write, but many felt it to be more necessary that they should be clothed and fed than that they should learn the dead languages. Parson Russell, being a graduate of the college at "Newtown," to which John Harvard left his library and fortune, was greatly desirous from the first that Hadley should have a grammar school, but there seemed no prospect that such a blessing could be secured. Nevertheless, in due time, through the legacy of Edward Hopkins, means were provided for the school so earnestly desired.

During Parson Russell's pastorate in Wethersfield, Edward Hopkins, the first secretary of the Colony of Connecticut, and its governor, was the most prominent figure in its social and political life. Born in England in 1600, this young Puritan came to Boston in 1637, in company with his close friend, Theophilus Eaton, afterward the first and only governor of the Colony of New Haven. Hopkins, although in very poor health, found himself at once pushed to the front and called upon to assist in the solution of problems of church and state. As a Commissioner of the United Colonies he signed in behalf of Connecticut the articles of confederation by which, in 1643, Massachusetts, Plymouth, Connecticut, and New Haven united under the name of the United Colonies of New England.

While living quietly in Hartford, Governor Hopkins continued his business as a merchant, pushed his trading stations up the river and into the wilderness, and founded the trade in American cotton, and all the time "conflicted with bodily infirmities which held him for thirty years together." He married Anna Yale, the daughter of the second wife of Theophilus Eaton, the widow of David Yale, after whose grandson, Elihu Yale, the college was named. Mrs. Hopkins was a literary woman who soon became insane, as the record runs, "by occasion of her giving herself wholly to reading and writing." We read further, "Her husband being very loving and tender, was loath to grieve her, but he saw his error when it was too late. For if she had attended her household affairs and such things as belong to women and not gone out of her way and calling to meddle in such things as are proper for men whose minds are stronger, she had kept her wits and might have improved them usefully and honorably in the place God had set her." This sad effect upon the female mind of too much study furnished the wise men of that day with another argument against the education of women, and brought lasting grief to the too indulgent husband, already wasted by disease.

In the midst of his career Edward Hopkins was suddenly called to England by the death of his brother. Parliamentary duties detained him in the mother country, his family joined him, and he died in London in 1657, two years before the "engagers" betook themselves and their convictions to the wilderness of Hadley. The will of Governor Hopkins, after making due provision for his "dear destressed wife" and other legacies, bequeathed the residue of his estate to Theophilus Eaton, John Davenport, John Cullick, and William Goodwin, "in full assurance of their trust and faithfulness in disposing of it according to the true intent of me, the said Edward Hopkins, which is to give some encouragement in those foreign plantations for the breeding of hopeful youths, both at the grammar school and college for the public service of the country in future times."

The will was made in England and "those foreign plantations" were the New England colonies. Mr. Eaton died soon after the will was made, as did also Captain Cullick, so that the disposition of the estate fell to Davenport and Goodwin. As Davenport was pastor in Boston, the chief burden fell upon Goodwin, who was a leader in the movement which resulted in the founding of Hadley. It was through his action that so large a part of the legacy was secured by the new settlement.

The Hampshire County court in probate, March 30, 1669, ratified an agreement whereby Parson John Russell, Jr., Samuel Smith, Aaron Cooke, Jr., Nathaniel Dickinson, and Peter Tilton were constituted trustees to act with William Goodwin, and after his decease to have full power to establish the school in Hadley and to manage its estates, including the Hopkins fund and all other property coming into its possession. Hadley's share of the Hopkins fund amounted to £308. More money was expected to come from England after the death of Mrs. Hopkins, but this was never secured by Hadley. The sum received was not considered sufficient to start and equip the grammar school. In recognition of this fact donations came in from citizens who, having no children of their own, desired to contribute toward so worthy an object for the benefit of future generations. John Barnard gave a part of Hockanum meadow and some of the "Greate Meadowe" and "a piece of land lying in the Forlorn"; and Nathaniel Ward, at whose home in Hartford the "engagers" held their memorable meeting, bestowed his house and home lot, and a piece of meadow land; while a few years later, Henry Clark left to the school his nine-acre lot in Hockanum, and his portion of the "Greate Meadowe." The town itself granted "two little meddowes next beyond the Brooke commonlie called the Mill Brooke" for the support of the school, and appointed Henry Clarke, Lieutenant Smith, William

Allis, Nathaniel Dickinson, Sr., and Andrew Warner as a committee in charge. These "school Meadows," containing about sixty acres, were in the northern part of the town, adjoining the river, and were separated by a high ridge on which was the Indian fort. From this time on the school in Hadley was known as the Hopkins grammar school, true to the intent of its benefactor.

There is no doubt but that the little children of the town were gathered in some good wife's kitchen that first winter of the settlement and were taught by a "school dame" first lessons from the hornbook and "New England Primer," but of such teaching no account has been preserved. The earliest record of any school in Hadley states that in 1665 it was "Voted by the Town that they would give 20 pound pr Annum for 3 yeares toward the maintenance of a Scoole master to teach children and to be as a helpe to Mr. Russell as occasion may require." This first "scoole master" was Mr. Caleb Watson, a Harvard graduate, who was in Hadley in 1667 and remained as teacher of the Hopkins school until 1673, when his very decided difference of opinion with Mr. Russell made it impossible for him longer to be a "helpe" in any capacity. His pupils met in the house presented by Goodman Ward, which stood on the site of the residence owned recently by L. S. Crosier. Probably a few girls were among the scholars, although remembering the fate of

Mrs. Edward Hopkins, parents must have feared the effect of too much learning upon their daughters, and guarded their "intellects" with zealous care. Girls were allowed to learn to read, but not to write, and that historic text-book, the Latin Accidence, was not for them to meddle with. Arithmetic was taught by oral methods, as books were rare, and until 1750 spelling books were unknown.

The following general regulations, recorded and enforced, kept parents to their duty, and children to their tasks.

"Allsoe with respect to the great ffailure of persons in not sending their children to scoole it is ordered and voted by the Town that the present Selectmen and the Selectmen Annuallye shall take a list of all the children six years ould to twelve, which shall be compellable if not sent to scoole to pay Annuallye according to and equallye with those that are Sent only some poore men's children which shall be exempted as they shall be judged by the Selectmen And ffrom six yeares ould to continue till twelve at scoole except they Attain a ripeness and dexteritie in Inferior learning, as writeing & reading which shall be Judged by the Scoolemaster."

Every Latin "Scollard" had to pay twenty shillings a year, and every English "Scollard" sixteen shillings. In 1677 Mr. John Younglove was the teacher with a salary of £30 a year, and a home lot on which to live. In 1680 the town voted to get a teacher "that shall

Hopkins Grammar School and Academy 81

teach the Latin Tongue as allsoe the English to any that are entered with writeing and Cyphering." In 1686 Samuel Partrigg was engaged to teach, and was paid £8 for his work. Warham Mather, son of the minister in Northampton, was followed in the school by Thomas Swan of Roxbury, John Morse of Dedham, Salmon Treat of Wethersfield, Joseph Smith, the son of Lieutenant Philip Smith, and John Hubbard.

When in 1698 Joseph Smith was again engaged, the town built the first schoolhouse, twenty-five by eighteen feet and seven feet between the joists, in the middle of the broad street. Deacon Simeon Dickinson, who died in 1890, aged ninety-five, remembered attending the Hopkins school when its sessions were held in this earliest building. Nathaniel Chauncey, the first graduate of Yale College, taught the school in 1702. Among those who came after him were Jonathan Marsh, John Partrigg, Aaron Porter, all Harvard graduates; and these were followed by Rev. Daniel Boardman, John James, and Elisha Williams of Hatfield, who afterward became president of Yale College. Stephen Williams of Deerfield, Ebenezer Gay of Dedham, Nathaniel Mather of Windsor, Stephen Steele of Hartford, Solomon Williams of Hatfield, Daniel Dwight of Northampton, Benjamin Dickinson of Hatfield, follow on the list, until in 1724 Israel Chauncey, the son of Rev. Isaac Chauncey, for a brief period ruled over the Hopkins school. Most of these who have been mentioned, and some who came later, were embryo ministers, college graduates or students in the midst of their college course. During all these years the Hopkins school had remained a classical grammar school, but the means by which its Greek and Latin courses had been preserved in the face of determined opposition require a separate narrative. The dogged determination with which these conscientious guardians of a sacred trust, with Parson Russell at their head, in the midst of poverty, discouragement, and Indian alarms, fought to keep the Hopkins school true to the spirit of its founder has been an object lesson for all trustees of public institutions since those strenuous days of struggle and of victory.

The trustees of the Hopkins fund found that the most profitable way in which to invest so large a sum of money was a problem to be solved. The building left by Goodman Ward could be used for a schoolhouse, and the meadow land given by the town and citizens would yield abundant crops, which could be handed over to the master. Elder Goodwin, in choosing his trustees, selected men of strong convictions, and those appointed by the town were no less able and efficient. There seems to have been clashing of wills from the first among the members of the board, but Goodwin ruled the day, and with the money built a gristmill on Mill River, south of the school lands, and the town granted a home lot for the miller. Then with the mill just finished, and the school just started, and the little town which he had labored to establish just gaining a foothold in the valley, Ruling Elder Goodwin abandoned the whole undertaking, packed his household goods, and in 1670 removed to Farmington, Conn., near to his former home.

It seems to have been impossible for Mr. Goodwin's determined will to brook opposition, and finding that men were of many minds in Hadley as well as in Hartford, he decided to give up the struggle as all men seemed to be against him. In bitterness of spirit he brought in 1672 a suit in the Springfield court against Peter Tilton and the other trustees for "intruding themselves upon the committeeship about ye estate of Edward Hopkins, improved in Hadley, contrary to the mind of the said Mr. Goodwin, trustee to the sd estate." The case was dismissed, and seven months later, in 1673, William Goodwin, the last Ruling Elder of Hadley, died a broken-hearted man.

The court commended his services in the following words:

"The Corte considering the admirable intenseness, the indefatigable care and paynes that Mr. Goodwin hath expressed to promote and advance the affairs of the scoole, both for its foundation and progress Doe thankfully accept thereof." "They acknowledge the good hand of God in sending those reverend fathers and worthy Gentlemen the said Trustees to dispose of such an estate to these remote parts of the country and of this colony, for so worthy and eminent a work."

Elder Goodwin's daughter Elizabeth remained in Hadley as the wife of John Crow. Deacon Rodney Smith, who died in Hadley in 1890, was a lineal descendant of William Goodwin.

Although it may have seemed that his endeavors in behalf of Hadley youth were not appreciated by his generation, the children of the town have in these later days reared to his memory a noble monument. Beneath the shadow of a patriarchal elm it stands, a handsome brick library building, containing beside the well selected volumes a room filled with curios and relics of old Hadley days. Here we see the interleaved almanacs in which Josiah Pierce traced his quaint records, a panel from the old first meeting-house, and many other articles rescued from the shadows of the past. Over the entrance appears the inscription, "This building was erected in the year 1902 in memory of Elder William Goodwin, one of the Hadley pioneers, by his descendant John Dwight, and other friends and citizens of the town."

The death of Elder Goodwin gave Parson Russell and the Hon. Peter Tilton each a chance to exercise his individuality in the management of school affairs, which soon became complicated by the outbreak of the Indian war. Being far beyond the stockade, the school mill was for two years protected by a small garrison until, one dark night in 1677, the people of Hadley saw the northern sky illumined by flames, and knew that the greater part of the school possessions were no more. Part of the mill-dam remained, but while the woods were lurking places for the enemy the town considered it useless to rebuild the mill, so the farmers again carried their grain to Hatfield, and the mill site was deserted. These were gloomy days for the Hopkins school, and Parson Russell must have seen his cherished vision of a flourishing classical institution and even of a college fade in the distance. But still he and his colleagues kept stout hearts, and faced the situation, not knowing that worse was yet to come.

Robert Boltwood, an influential Hadley pioneer, cast longing glances at the water power going to waste at the ruined dam of the school mill, and taking advantage of the decline of grammar school interest among the people boldly declared he was not afraid of Indians, and offered the town £10 for the site and remains of the dam. The bargain was completed, and in 1678 Boltwood built his mill, and equipped it with millstones of red sandstone brought from the brow of Mt. Tom. We can imagine the disappointment of Parson Russell at this action, and his indignation at the prevailing indifference toward the classical course in the school. The Hopkins money had been put into the mill, and the mill was burned. The remainder of the school funds having been given by Hadley people, and their desire being to have an English school, the matter seemed practically settled. March 30, 1680, Parson Russell called the attention of the county court to "the languishing estate of the school." His plea that the mill ought to belong to the school was presented with so much eloquence that the court decided that it should "not allow of so great a wrong," and ordered that the town should pay Boltwood what he had spent in rebuilding, and restore the mill to the trustees.

In 1682 the exchange had not been made. Philip Smith had been elected to the board of trustees in the place of his father, and to their future sorrow the remaining trustees had chosen Samuel Partrigg in the place of Peter Tilton, resigned. Russell and Cooke, for the trustees, appeared in the Springfield court and told the whole story, describing the lands and moneys received, the moneys spent for cellar and "craine" and chimney and oven and house over mill and "Damm," the income of £26 a year derived from the mill, and the tragic manner in which their grammar school had vanished into thin air. Samuel Partrigg, a man of great wealth and influence, favored the English school. With this disaffection within the board itself the case was hard indeed! Parson Russell pleaded, and wrote letters, and urged the matter until even his courage failed. Some question of title stood in the

Hopkins Grammar School and Academy 87

way, and matters rested there. In 1683 Robert Boltwood agreed to give up the mill for £138 in grain and pork. Then Robert died and Samuel his son would not fulfil his father's bargain.

Parties of influence outside of Hadley felt much sympathy for Parson Russell as he thus battled almost alone for the classical school so dear to his heart. October, 1686, John Pynchon, in a letter to Mr. Russell, said:

"I am hartily sorry Mr. Partrigg is so cross in ye businesse of the school." "Nothing will be done as it ought to be until he be removed, wh I suppose the Predt and Council may do." "Mr. Tilton fully falling in with him, is as full and strong in all his notions as Mr. P. himself." "Mr. Tilton said it would kindle such a flame yt would not be quenched. But if to do right and secure public wright kindle a flame, the will of the Ld. be done."

November 19, 1686, a town-meeting was called in Hadley, "when the sun was a quarter of an hour high," to consider school matters. Captain Aaron Cooke and Joseph Hawley, sent to examine into the school situation, after wearisome waiting, received from Tilton and Partrigg, a committee from the town, a report that there was "no complaint." Then the school committee appeared, and Parson Russell, quoting scripture, gave seven long reasons why the school moneys must be used for a grammar school. Partrigg in reply also quoted scripture and said, "He that can teach Grammar is surely better fitted to teach English than he that hath no Grammar in him."

Finally the town committee clinched the argument by declaring that an English school must as a matter of fact be a grammar school. The council dismissed Mr. Partrigg, and a committee of arbitration decided that Samuel Boltwood should be paid for what he and his father had expended for the mill, and that the property should be delivered to the trustees of the Hopkins fund "for the maintenance of the school to which it belongs." The last clause was open to almost any construction, and a paper passed through the town for signatures disclosed the fact that only eleven men and one woman believed that the school in question should be a grammar school instead of an English school.

But the hard-fought battle for the continuance of classical instruction in Hadley was won, and the mill passed into the hands of the trustees, who used the income for the grammar school until the great flood of 1692 swept the whole structure away down the stream. The mill was presently rebuilt, and for a time John Clary was the miller, and after him Joseph Smith and his son Benjamin, and grandsons Erastus, Caleb, and Benjamin. The rent was used for the support of the school, which throughout the quarrel had kept up its regular sessions.

Hopkins Grammar School and Academy   89

In 1720 the school committee, as the board of trustees was now called, consisted of Chileab Smith, Thomas Hovey, Samuel Porter, Sergt. Joseph Smith, and Deacon John Smith. In 1733 the record states:

"We the subscribers, Lieutenant Westwood Cooke, Lieut. John Smith, and Eleazer Porter of the Scool Committy in Hadley have made Choyce of Deacon Samuel Dickinson to serve as a committy man in the room and sted of Lieut. Thomas Hovey, one of the scool Committy, he being aged and crazy and declines the service any longer. And we have also made Choyce of Mr. Job Marsh to serve as a Committy man in the room and sted of Mr. Joseph Smith, one of our late scool committy men now deceast."

Thus one by one the older members of the school committee dropped away and their successors were chosen by those who still remained. Moses Cooke, Deacon Joseph Eastman, "Ensine" Moses Marsh, Deacon Enos Nash, Samuel Gaylord, David Smith, Elisha Porter, Edmund Hubbard, Charles Phelps, Oliver Smith, Enos Nash, and Elisha Dickinson each took his turn in looking after the interests of the Hopkins grammar school. Sometimes the committee lent the town the money to pay the teacher, so that it seemed a little doubtful by whom he was engaged, but so long as he continued to teach the "Latin Accidence" it made but little difference.

In 1743 the school committee, Eleazer Porter,

Westwood Cooke, John Smith, Samuel Dickinson, and Job Marsh, engaged Josiah Pierce of Woburn, a graduate of Harvard in 1735, to teach the Hopkins school, and unlike the short terms of his predecessors, his administration lasted until 1755. His home was on the present site of the church and town hall. His salary of £27½ a year, with the use of twenty-five acres of land, and a pittance gained by serving as town clerk, kept his family in comfort. Although not a minister he occasionally supplied a pulpit, for which he received ten shillings a Sunday. The entries in his interleaved almanac have given us many facts about those old school days in Hadley. Somehow the selectmen lost their grip upon both pupils and parents, for Mr. Pierce had sometimes five and sometimes thirty scholars in his school, and children came or not as they and their parents pleased. One day the record reads, "No school because no scholars sent." November 19, 1742, we find this entry:

"This day being the day before Thanksgiving I keep school all day as I have heretofore, willing to attend; if parents will let their children attend; but they the most of them, letting their children play about the streets rather than send them to school, I determine not to attend ye school in ye afternoon of such day hereafter."

After twelve years of service Mr. Pierce left Hadley to teach in Northampton and South Hadley, but in

1760 he returned and was again for six years the teacher of the grammar school. Afterwards he kept a "cyphering school" in Amherst until obliged to close it for want of wood. This veteran school teacher knew some things beside the lore of books, for in 1763 he showed the Hadley farmers how to raise a new crop, that of potatoes, red in color and not at first considered as fit to be eaten. Eight bushels of this queer sort of "root" Josiah Pierce put into his cellar that first winter, and three years later his crop was sixty bushels. After a time he seems to have found raising potatoes more profitable than drilling Latin verbs into the minds of stupid scholars, for we see him no more in the schoolroom, and three hundred bushels of potatoes produced upon his land in 1769 supplied the whole town. Josiah Pierce died in 1788, having made his record not only as a teacher of the dead languages but also as an agriculturist far in advance of his time.

The first day of the new year, 1816, was memorable in Hadley. In a town-meeting held that morning it was voted to ask the General Court that the Hopkins fund should be devoted to the maintenance of an academy for the benefit not only of Hadley but of the surrounding towns as well. This petition was granted. The people were now united in their desire for a preparatory school, and the wisdom of Parson Russell's policy was vindicated by the descendants of those who fought so bitterly against it. The trustees of the grammar school, Seth Smith, William Porter, Jacob Smith, William Dickinson, and Moses Porter, after the incorporation of the academy was complete, chose Rev. Dan Huntington, Rev. John Woodbridge, Rev. Joseph Lyman, and Isaac C. Bates as additional members of the board, and began to make plans for a new academy building. Part of the home lot of Chester Gaylord was secured as a site. Many persons contributed building material, supplies, and labor, and others gave from fifty to eighty cents in money, and so the work went on. Another year saw a fine three-storied brick building on the site of the academy building of to-day. It was an elegant structure for a rural town, and people came to see it from all the country round. Its entire cost was $4,954.90. December 9, 1817, the new building was dedicated. Rev. Joseph Lyman of Hatfield made the prayer, and Rev. John Woodbridge preached the sermon from the text, "And thou shalt teach them diligently unto thy children." The first school session in the new building was held September 10, 1817, with Rev. Dan Huntington, preceptor, Giles Crouch Kellogg and Miss Sophia Moseley, assistants. The next year Mr. Huntington received $500 salary, Mr. Kellogg $20 a month, and Miss Sally Williston $12 a month and board.

The new school building fronted on the middle lane, and the main entrance opened at first directly upon the sidewalk, but soon the trustees were allowed to enclose part of the lane for a school-yard. Two classrooms occupied the lower floor, and five rooms, used for recitations and to contain scientific apparatus and the beginning of a library, occupied the second floor. The spacious third story, known as Academy Hall, was the pride of the town. At the east end, on the stage four feet above the floor, embryo orators spouted poetry, and read compositions at the Wednesday afternoon rhetorical exercises, to the edification of admiring friends. Here debates were held on abstruse subjects, exhibitions were given, lecturers spoke words of wisdom, and diplomas were awarded to those who had attained a "ripeness and dexteritie" in all sorts of learning. Truly the days of prosperity for classical education, so fondly dreamed of by Parson Russell, were at last realized by Hopkins Academy, the daughter of the grammar school.

The funds in the hands of the academy trustees, the year the school was opened, were increased by a grant from the General Court of half a township in Maine, which was sold, the proceeds being turned into the school treasury. The academy prospered greatly, ninety-nine students, sixty-five from Hadley, being enrolled the second year. Tuition was from three dollars to three dollars and a half a quarter, and board, including room rent and washing, was one dollar and a half a week. Those whose necessities required it found work to help defray their expenses. All pupils were compelled to attend church and prayer meeting and the Bible was a most important text-book. Mr. Huntington was the preceptor until 1821. Other preceptors were Rev. Worthington Smith, D.D., afterward the president of the University of Vermont, Oliver S. Taylor, who died in 1885 aged one hundred years, Rev. John A. Nash, who came to Amherst and established Nash's school, George Nichols, afterward rector of Hopkins' Grammar School in New Haven, Timothy Dwight, of the class of 1827 in Amherst College, and Rev. Ezekiel Russell, D.D., Amherst College, 1829, who became pastor of Olivet Church, Springfield.

In the early days of Hopkins Academy four of the principals each found a wife among the assistant teachers. In 1831 one hundred and fifty young men and one hundred and twenty-one young women were enrolled among the students, one hundred and forty-eight of these being from out of town. The fame of the academy extended west and south, and pupils from Ohio, Georgia, Virginia, Alabama, and Florida entered to prepare for college. In 1831 the question arose as to the rights of the trustees to allow the benefits of the school to extend to so many outside of the town, and the matter was taken into court and decided in favor of the trustees. As free high schools became common, academies everywhere declined, and the institution in Hadley suffered with the rest. Finally in 1851 began the last controversy about the Hopkins

Hopkins Grammar School and Academy 95

fund, when in town-meeting Samuel Nash, Esq., Dr. Bonney, and P. S. Williams, Esq., were appointed a committee to see if the school could not be made free to the town. Year after year the matter was brought up, discussed, and left undecided. The trustees claimed that "the town has no more exclusive rights to the funds of the Hopkins Academy than to those of any other literary institution," and that "the trustees believe that it is the best for all concerned that the charter of our academy remain unmolested." At last in 1860 fate seemed against the trustees, for the academy building, on which no insurance had been placed, was destroyed by fire.

Then came the opportunity of the town. March 26, 1860, it was voted:

"Whereas, in the Providence of God, the Academy building has been destroyed by fire and thereby a favorable opportunity presented to the town for an effort to make available to all the inhabitants of the town the benefits of the school fund which was given by the town and by benevolent individuals for the promotion and advancement of learning; therefore, voted; that the town will erect a building suitable for the accomodation of a Free High School, provided the trustees will enter into an arrangement and agreement with the town that they will appropriate the annual income of the fund to aid in support of such school."

The trustees, though at a disadvantage, were still loth to give up their charter, and clung to the name

"Hopkins Academy." When finally overpersuaded, they insisted that the new high school should be built on the site of the old academy. The town objected, and a board of arbitration, to which the matter was submitted, stood five to five, and there the matter rested.

For two years school was kept in the basement of the church. In 1862 Levi Stockbridge, Horace Cook, and Theodore Huntington were added to the board of trustees, and the offer was made that if the town would pay $300, the school should be free to Hadley pupils for one year. This proposition was accepted, and five years after the first vote was taken the subject of a high school building was again cautiously introduced, and at last it was voted to place it on the site of the old academy. The triumph of the trustees was thus made complete. Hopkins Academy of ancient lineage was thenceforth to be a school free to all pupils of the town able to meet the entrance requirements.

During these years the school meadows had been gathering Hatfield soil washed over by the river, which made a new channel and thus created an island. This finally was added to the mainland, and thus the sixty acres first given by the town became in 1844 a hundred and fifty-eight acres, which the trustees were granted leave to sell, thereby increasing the fund to $57,325. The mill privilege at North Hadley was sold to L. N. Granger for $300. The trustees in 1890 owned ten acres of land on Mount Holyoke, eleven in Hockanum

Hopkins Grammar School and Academy

Meadow, four and a half in Aqua Vitæ Meadow, five in the Great Upper Landing, two in the Great Lower Landing, besides sundry investments in stocks and mortgages.

Many graduates of this famous old academy have preached the gospel throughout the earth. Jeremiah Porter was a home missionary on the western frontier. Elijah C. Bridgman and James G. Bridgman carried the good news to China. Dyer Ball went out to Singapore. John Dunbar was a teacher among the Pawnee Indians. Dwight W. Marsh and Lyman Bartlett were sent to Turkey, and Henry M. Bridgman was a pioneer missionary in South Africa. A long list of ministers, thirty doctors, twenty-five lawyers, are included in the roll of honor. Among the eminent educators we find William D. Whitney of Yale, Levi Stockbridge, president of the agricultural college at Amherst, Professor Richard H. Mather of Amherst College, President L. Clark Seelye of Smith College. Thirty-eight ministers secured their wives among the Hopkins alumni, and in this list we find Miss Eunice Bullard, who married Henry Ward Beecher. Major General Joseph Hooker and General Joseph B. Plummer are among those educated in the Hopkins school who served their country in the civil war. Verily old Parson Russell and his colleagues who established and maintained the integrity of the grammar school in Hadley builded better than they knew.

CHAPTER V

THE WEALTH OF THE RIVER AND THE FERTILE MEADOWS

FAR up among the northern hills the brimming waters of two crystal fountains united in a tiny rivulet, which trickled southward toward the sea. "Heart Lake" and "Double Lake" through which it passed paid tribute, and four rippling mountain brooks hastened to swell the stream. Now dashing over rocks and boulders, now broken into roaring cataracts, now flowing in a somber sheet within the shadow of rugged mountain peaks, with steady persistence the river shaped its course. Salmon and sturgeon leaped amid its rapids, and wild birds skimmed its shining surface. Flocks of pigeons, pausing in their flight, whitened the shores, and timid deer drank undisturbed the clear and sparkling waters. Beside the river, all along the way, solemn pine forests guarded curve and shallow, while single trees on bank and hilltop kept untiring watch. The summer breeze blew softly through these dark woods, and tiny blossoms peeped timidly up through crevices in the brown carpet of dry pine needles. No sign of civilization marred the freshness

The Connecticut River and the Meadow Plain
Looking North from the Railroad

of the picture. The native hunter as he glided in his light canoe from shore to shore seemed closely akin to the creatures of the woods and waters. This undiscovered country was the red man's heritage and his ancestral home.

The Indians christened their river "Quinnetuk," the long river with waves. "Quonektacut" was applied in later years to include both the stream and the land along its shores. The little rill from the north, its tortuous journey over, found at last its outlet, and four hundred miles from its source poured a mighty flood into Long Island Sound. In place of mountain cliff and rocky headland, pebbly beaches and sloping grassy banks and open meadow lands added new beauty to the smiling landscape. But still the dark pine forests, untouched by woodman's ax, crowned every eminence, and clung persistently wherever they could find a foothold. Therefore the Indian added to the harsh word "Quonektacut" the poetic title "River of Pines." This name has long since been forgotten. The grim and gloomy pines which gave the words their meaning disappeared before the settlers' rude attack, and the river Indians themselves vanished to make way for the colonist and his civilization. A few dry bones and arrow heads are all that remain of these ancient owners of the Connecticut valley. The romance of the river has departed and its tale is still untold.

This historic stream was a most important factor in the settlement of the valley towns. When Indian trails were the only traveled paths and highways were unknown, this natural waterway formed a connecting link between the isolated villages by means of which they were kept in touch with each other and in communication with the outside world. The founders of Hadley knew the river as a somewhat fickle friend, which in its angry moods proved a serious menace to all within its reach. In early spring the frozen highway was suddenly transformed into a roaring torrent. A moving ice floe from the north swept down with irresistible force and miniature icebergs ground against each other with savage fury and were pounded to fragments among the rocks and rapids. Then, a mighty flood, the swollen river spread far over the meadows, and, receding, left a deposit of rich soil which would produce a bountiful yield of hay and grain. The colonist loved his river in all its moods. He built his house where, from the open door, he could discern its shining surface. In time of inundation he kept his canoe fastened to the door-post, and until the water entered the dwelling refused to leave his home. When he discovered that the fickle stream by cutting through a neck of land had in a night removed a portion of his estate to a neighboring town, still with an unconquered spirit the valley farmer met these new conditions, subdued the forces of nature and taught them to become his servants, refused to be driven from the land of his adoption, and is buried to-day beside the river in the beautiful valley where he delighted to dwell.

The Hadley housewife found the river a means of supplying her larder when other sources failed. Game became scarce upon the mountains and in 1698 the State enacted laws for the protection of deer. In 1740 Westwood Cooke, Samuel Rugg, and John Nash served Hadley as "Deer Reeves," and received for the detection of each guilty hunter half the fine imposed for killing game contrary to law. Even wild turkeys finally disappeared, but fish was always plentiful and free to all alike. So every Hadley farmer became a fisherman, and seine and scoop-net his implements of toil. The first settlers found shad and salmon in abundance. Believing that things of value were only to be secured by means of time and labor, for many years the citizens cared little for the food so easily obtained and were ashamed when caught with fish upon their tables. Pork was their medium of exchange, and to be eating fish implied a scarcity of pork and a state of poverty to be deplored. Then salmon were taken into favor, and shad, when scooped by mistake, were thrown back into the river. After many years the fashion changed and shad became a favorite food and salmon were discarded. One old Hadley resident who had the courage to declare that shad are very good whether one has any pork or not was said to have a "very peculiar taste." But whatever the opinion, when game became scarce the people were thankful to take the food provided without question or complaint. The thought that fish could be worth money did not at first enter their minds, and there has been found no record of the sale of shad before 1733.

In 1715 the General Court made an additional grant of a tract of land four miles square to the township of Hadley, so that the town should thereafter include within its limits what is now South Hadley and South Hadley Falls and control the fishing privilege at the "Greate Falls" on the east side of the river. Three other excellent fishing places, one below the mouth of Mill River, one a little east of the southern end of the same river, and another near Hockanum Meadow, belonged especially to Hadley. Forty salmon, weighing between thirty and forty pounds each, were caught in one day near the second of these places, and here Enos Lyman took three thousand one hundred and forty fish in one prodigious haul. Josiah Pierce and six other Hadley men owned a seine together in 1766, and sold shad for a penny apiece. The first dam at South Hadley Falls made it difficult for the salmon to ascend the river, so that after 1800 few were caught in the upper stream.

The settlers, having learned from the Indians their method of taking fish from the rocks at the "Greate

Falls," devised improvements as facilities increased. Each spring time crowds of men and boys hastened to this famous fishing place to gather in the bounty of the river. The first of May became a sort of picnic season, anticipated through the long winter by those to whom vacations were unknown. Life was one tedious work day of interminable hours, so that the youth of Hadley hailed with joy an excuse for anything like recreation. With the approach of the shad season nets and other fishing implements were repaired, and all was made ready for the great event of the year. When April showers had melted the snows which had made the roads impassable, a straggling procession climbed the hills and struggled through the mud with all faces turned toward the "Greate Falls." Here were men on horseback with bags in which to load their fish, and here a farmer rode in his cart, and again a horseman led another horse provided to carry the load. Many brought provisions intending to camp upon the river bank, and others sought accommodation in homes along the way. Hadley inns thus became crowded, and private houses were filled with guests. From the middle of April until toward the first of June all Hampshire County went a fishing. Fifteen hundred horses were sometimes tied to the trees in the vicinity of the Falls, where their owners were either buying or catching fish. Below the Falls men were drawing in the seines, and from boats fastened to the rocks were taking in the shad with scoopnets, while others were spearing sturgeon or making bargains with those who came to buy. At nightfall Hadley fishermen hastened homeward, but others from a distance camped beside the falls, and after dark, by the light of flaring torches, caught great lamprey eels which in the hill towns were much esteemed for food. Frolicsome boys enjoyed the sport of wading in the water after dark, and by the flaring torchlight, with the hand protected by a coarse yarn mitten, picked up the eels and carried them to the shore. Light and trifling youngsters spent the evening in wrestling and trials of skill, with glasses of rum for refreshment, but such sports were few and were frowned upon severely. After the fishing season fresh fish were daily on the family table, and quantities were cured for winter use, until, for self-protection, hired men, in making a contract, stipulated that they should be obliged to eat only a certain amount of salted shad.

Next to the fisheries, after the Revolution, lumbering became of great importance to the valley towns. All along the shore new villages were springing up, and with the progress of civilization came the downfall of the forests. After the peace with the Indians in 1726, great logs of pine, cut in the far north by a company of Connecticut and Massachusetts men, floated down the river on the way to the king's contractor in Boston, who purchased them for the masts of British vessels.

Agents of the king in every town kept watch and seized all logs of the required size, claiming them by virtue of the "Pine Tree Laws," which were very offensive to the people. After the Revolution pine trees were cut and sent to market without restriction. Timber was by this time scarce in Hadley, and tradition says that more than once logs which lodged in a farmer's dooryard were built into his new house with the excuse that being on his land they were his property. Many difficulties arose between the lumbermen and farmers, the former bringing suit against the latter for stopping their logs, and the latter making complaint for the damage done to their meadows. Rafting was found to be more practicable than floating single logs, and often in the spring the river would be full of rafts, propelled by ponderous oars. With creak and groan and shouts of warning from the oarsmen, the great flotilla, laden with shingles and clapboards, swept on with the grandeur of an army corps, waking the echoes from the mountain sides, and calling the inhabitants to see the wondrous sight. The life of the lumberman was a series of adventures. Embarking near the head waters of the stream, exposed to storm and stress of weather, floating past forests infested by wild beasts, tossing through rapids and wedged between great rocks and stranded in sand and shallows, he shaped his tortuous course, and by skilful steering reached at last the haven of his hopes. Rafts of boards could thus be transported over the falls, but sawed lumber had to be carted, so in 1765 the "Lumber Road" was built, two and a half miles in length, from above the falls to the landing below the rapids. Near this road, in the Falls Field and Falls Wood, were three sawmills and a tavern kept by Titus Pomeroy, and afterward there was another, the property of Daniel Lamb. The farmers of the vicinity, changing their occupation, became carriers of lumber, and the Hadley landing-place, taken from John Chapin's farm, was a scene of great activity.

The island which had formed below Fort Meadow, not belonging to any one, was observed with envious eyes. One season the grass was cut by a Hadley citizen named Brooks, and when he came to get his hay, behold it was not there, being safely stowed away in the barn of Nathaniel Day across the river. In 1770 the General Court sold the island to Solomon Stoddard, who made a bargain for half of it with Noah Edwards, and in 1803 Levi Shepherd bought the whole of it for $1,200.

Commerce and articles of exchange increased, and the Hadley farmer, not satisfied to raft and cart his shingles, loading and unloading at much expense of time and labor, felt that the problem of more rapid river transportation must at once be solved. Though at intervals great rocks and rapids threatened destruction to any who attempted passage, and shoals and shallows wrought daily changes in the channel, nevertheless those sturdy pioneers, having subdued the wilderness, were not to be discouraged by waterfalls and sandbars. Vast projects for improvements shaped themselves within the public mind and were expressed through the public press.

By strenuous efforts the settlers had been able from the first to carry on some traffic with their friends in the upper valley, and thus secure many things needful for their comfort. "Greate Canoes," laden with three or four tons of "Flower" and "Porke" and beaver skins, and managed by two men, were the first freight boats to run the rapids, but the passage was both difficult and dangerous. Then came the "Falls Boats," a kind of shipping now extinct. These were of two kinds: "Pine Boats," twenty-five tons burden, with neither cabin nor floor, and "Oak Boats," which were fitted up with comfortable accommodations for the crew. The tiny cabin, lighted with four windows, was warmed by a cook stove, and provided with four bunks, which in the daytime were turned up against the side of the boat. A mainmast, topmast, mainsail and topsail, made it possible to take advantage of the slightest wind, and there were two pairs of stout oars with which, when breezes failed, the boat could be moved along. Loaded with farm produce, shingles, ash plank, furs, and fish, these unwieldy vessels would move slowly down the river, assisted through the rapids and over the falls by experienced pilots who lived along the shore. How the boys and girls must have shouted and the women have run to the doors to see the Dispatch, or the Flying Fish, or the Clinton, or the Vermont come sailing bravely by! The name of each vessel, painted outside its cabin in large black letters, was scanned with interest from the shore, and many a farmer hailed the boatman to learn the news from up the river, or ask for transportation for something he had to sell.

Having no keel, these Falls Boats slipped over rocks and sandbars and without much difficulty reached their destination, delivered their cargoes, and were loaded again with all the various goods in the country store for use by the farmer and his family. Then came a time of trial. All those weary miles the heavily laden boat was poled up stream, with ash poles, assisted sometimes by the wind but more often in a perfect calm. Poling was the hardest work known and caused much lameness and blistering of the skin in front of the shoulder, for which a frequent application of rum was a remedy. An old writer says, "It was also thought well to take some inside." When the boat reached the rapids in its progress up the stream, either it was hitched to an ox team on shore, or several men would take the place of oxen. Reaching smooth water, and aided by a friendly breeze, it would dash onward at the furious speed of five miles an hour toward the

Wealth of River and Fertile Meadows

next obstruction in the river. "Then," says the old writer, "the heart of the boatman rejoiced within him and the river bank echoed his songs of cheer, while the tired husbandman stood still and listened as the song and the voice passed by."

In 1792 the General Court passed an act incorporating a company entitled, "The Proprietors of the Locks and Canals on Connecticut River." Great excitement prevailed at South Hadley Falls, where the first attempt at digging a canal was made. Gun powder was the only explosive known, and drilling was done by the hands of men. Outside parties contributed funds, and at last a dam was constructed, and the work went slowly on. Two miles and a half through solid rock the channel for the canal was cut. The water, flooding the adjacent meadows, produced fever and ague and indignant citizens clamored for the removal of the dam. Those interested in the fisheries demanded a fishway that the shad might go up the river to their spawning shoals. The "Proprietors," however, persisted in their undertaking. December, 1794, the work was so nearly completed that a day of celebration was appointed, and many men and women were allowed to ride in the great car up and down the inclined plane. South Hadley Falls was now the most interesting place in the Connecticut valley, and hundreds of sightseers came on horseback to view this wonderful engineering feat, supposed to be of immense advantage to all engaged in transportation on the river.

Hadley had now completed its first century and was a veteran among New England towns. The primitive dwellings had been replaced by comfortable homes. Double rows of English elms, the patriarchs of to-day, planted on either side of the broad street, were growing straight and tall. The fertile meadows bore yearly their autumnal harvest of hay and grain. Wheat, rye, and barley flourished on the uplands, and great fields of Indian corn, that native product of the soil, furnished the farmer and his family with the hasty pudding which was his staple food. Josiah Pierce had taught his neighbors how to raise potatoes, but turnips were liked much better. The women made from flax the cloth for garments, bed clothing, and table linen, and, adding wool to flax, made linsey-woolsey for dresses, and to be exchanged for household utensils and imported stuff for gowns.

Levi Dickinson, a native of Wethersfield, who came to Hadley in 1786 and settled on the "Back Street," brought with him a queer new kind of "corn seed," which he showed his friends, saying that when fully grown it would make better brooms than they had ever seen. Hearing this, the Hadley housewife laughed him to scorn. "Husk brooms," to sweep the ovens, and "splinter brooms" made of birchen boughs, were good enough for every day, while the bristle and hair brooms, brought from England, certainly could not be surpassed by a farmer with any kind of corn. Thus reasoned the incredulous and argued not the case. Levi Dickinson, however, not discouraged, kept his own council, harvested the first crop of broom corn from his garden, contrived a method of scraping the seed from the brush with a knife, and afterward with the edge of a hoe, and sitting in a chair with the twine in a roll under his feet wound it around the brush in his lap and thus made brooms. Not asking his neighbors to buy, in 1798 he peddled his brooms in Williamsburg, Ashfield, and Conway, and said that the day when he sold his first broom was the happiest day of his life. In 1799 he carried brooms to Pittsfield and in 1800 as far as New London.

Then Hadley people began to realize that a new and profitable industry had been started in their midst. Cato, a colored man, planted some broom corn in the meadow, and William Shipman, Solomon Cooke, and Levi Gale began to raise the corn and manufacture brooms. Men in Hatfield and Whately went into the business, and Levi Dickinson, smiling to himself, calmly drove his teams loaded with brooms to Boston and to Albany and found a ready market. Making his own handles and spinning the twine from his own flax, the cost of the broom was little and the demand for the finished product was great. In 1810, 70,000 brooms were made in Hampshire County, and before the death of Levi Dickinson in 1843 people in all parts of the country were using Hadley brooms, and his triumph against local prejudice was complete. Broom corn had been cultivated for its seed in southern Europe, and a small amount was raised in the southern states, but the credit of planting it in large quantities and supplying the whole country with brooms belongs to Levi Dickinson. In 1850 Eleazer Porter, who took the census, reported forty-one broom factories and 769,700 brooms and 76,000 brushes produced in a single year within the limits of the little town of Hadley.

The canal had served its purpose in part when steamboats began to be used for transportation, and Hadley people were led to hope that they too might have a share in the benefits of this marvelous invention. The citizens longed and watched and listened for the little towboat Barnet, built in New York to ply upon the river. When, after many failures to ascend Enfield Falls, she was hauled bodily over the rocks and really appeared around Hockanum Bend, propelled by the wondrous power of steam, the people made a great rush to get on board the barge which she had in tow, and thus secure a share in this novel excursion. Then came the memorable flood, when travelers were taken in boats from Hadley Street across the meadows to Northampton, and buildings, trunks of trees, ruins of mills, bridges and fences, hay, pumpkins, apples, and cackling hens came dashing down the stream to be landed along the shore. The river itself seemed to resent invasion by this puffing, wheezing monster of steam and took revenge on all within its reach.

The steamer Vermont next started out from Hartford, bound for the Green Mountain State. Her passengers exclaimed with delight at the beauty of the scenery as she passed within the shadow of Titan's Pier, where columnar rocks rise high above the water's edge. Here was the abode of Manitou, the Great Spirit, and here two Indians were pursued and driven off the cliff to find death in the unknown depths below. Just beyond, to gain a few rods in distance, the vessel was compelled to travel four miles through the Ox Bow. The grandeur of those majestic mountains, valued chiefly as "woodlots" by farmers of the valley, impressed the strangers from the south, who gazed with surprise at the primitive hotel, kept by Willis Pease of Hadley, which, on the high summit of Mount Holyoke, appeared against the glowing sky. Past Stoddard's Island, over School Meadow Flats, beneath the sandstone cliff of Sugar Loaf, toward the green hills of her namesake state, steamed the Vermont, creating the hope that passenger traffic on the river had at last really commenced.

The summer of 1831 the steamboat William Hall left Hadley for Hartford three times a week, connecting with steamers for New York. Those were gala days for Hadley, but alas, the fates seemed unpropitious, and though many small steamboats were built and put into commission, yet the steamboat company failed, boilers burst, the shoals and currents shifted, and floods destroyed the work of years in a single night. One wintry morning, February 25, 1840, the people of Hockanum were surprised to find that the river had worn away the neck of the peninsula and cut a new channel for itself, thus making an island of three hundred acres of land, owned by Hadley farmers and worth thousands of dollars.

The reign of the steamboat could not be prolonged, for the day of the railroad was near at hand. July 4, 1845, the steamer Franklin left the wharf at Hadley, with two hundred people on board, "from the beauty and chivalry of West Street," bound for Montague. There they passed the day, enjoyed a picnic dinner with speeches and music, and returned in safety. This is the last we hear of steamboating at Hadley. That same year the people, crossing the toll bridge, could board the train behind the engine "Holyoke" and jolt away toward Springfield and the south. Opponents of the railroad became reconciled as its usefulness in carrying freight became understood. One enthusiast even found the railroad picturesque, and viewing the spring freshet from the tower of the church wrote thus to the Hampshire Gazette:

"The swollen river lay spread out at our feet in broad expanse, while scarce raised above the flood, the long straight line of railroad extended, and the ponderous train flying o'er it seemed like some huge sea bird, skimming the yielding wave with tireless wing."

Years later the Boston & Maine Railroad, passing through Hadley, connected Northampton with the capital city of the state, and since then the trolley has given Hadley citizens freedom to choose their ways and means of travel. The "huge sea bird" of iron and steam still flies over the "yielding wave" when the river overflows its meadows, but the river steamer is a thing of the past. The Pine Boats and Oak Boats, the captains and pilots, are unknown to the present generation. The scream of the locomotive echoes from the mountain sides, and all along the shore the trolley cars rush wildly seeking for their prey. The romance of the river has departed, its quiet and seclusion are invaded, its great pine forests are destroyed. Yet, unconquered, it takes its tortuous course, refusing to be curbed, impossible to control, declining to be improved, a wilful stream the same in nature as when the white man first gazed upon its waters.

To-day, as summer travelers admire the beauties of the Connecticut, the prosaic sunlight leaves little for imagination to feed upon. Yet, when beneath the midnight moon all discordant sounds have for a moment ceased, through the winding sheet of mist which hovers over the river's surface we fancy we catch the echoing dip of a shadowy paddle, and discern a light canoe darting from shore to shore. The unquiet ghost of some old Indian boatman has returned to haunt the valley and stream which were his ancient heritage. Again the river banks are clothed with dark pine forests, and from their depths the deer come down to drink and all is quiet sylvan beauty. The River of Pines is again a reality. To him whose eyes have been unsealed, for this magic moment the old days have returned.

The Hadley Cemetery

CHAPTER VI

THE BURIAL PLACE OF HADLEY'S HONORED DEAD

WITHIN the limits of the little river town, during the long years of effort and accomplishment, there had grown up another settlement, — the Hamlet of the Dead. Here, in 1661, on the Meadow Plain, near the home lot of Edward Church, the body of an unnamed infant of Philip Smith, grandchild of Lieutenant Samuel Smith, the first settler, was buried without prayer or service. A few months later Governor John Webster was in the same rude fashion, near the grave of the nameless child, placed beneath the sod. This was the beginning of Old Hadley cemetery, and here within the area of two hundred and ten square rods of rolling upland were buried for more than one hundred and thirty years all who died in Hadley.

Some sort of stone must have been placed at the grave of Governor Webster, for when in 1812 Noah Webster, his descendant in the fifth generation, came to live in Amherst, he had no difficulty in finding the resting-place of his distinguished ancestor, and erected above the same a monument to his memory, that bears the following words:

"To the memory of John Webster, Esq., one of the first settlers of Hartford in Connecticut, who was many years magistrate, or assistant and afterwards Deputy Governor and Governor of the colony, and in 1659 with three sons, Robert, William and Thomas associated with others in the purchase and settlement of Hadley, where he died in 1665."

The date here given, which is four years later than that given by the historian and genealogist, was probably indistinct upon the old stone, and therefore copied incorrectly.

This burial-place remained as Nature had left it during all those early years. No attempt at improvement or formal laying out of grounds was made, but, as overcome by disease, or slain by Indians, or worn to death by hard and constant toil, the weary workers ceased their labors, they were laid to rest beneath the pines and cedars and the life of the town went on as before. Nathaniel Ward, whose death occurred soon after that of Governor Webster, left his empty house a bequest to Hadley youth. John Hawkes and Thomas Stanley were the next of the first settlers to be carried on the shoulders of their fellow townsmen to their last long home. John Barnard, Richard Church, Stephen Terry, William Westwood, William Partrigg, and Andrew Bacon died in close succession, and Thomas Coleman followed them in 1674. Henry Clark, the patron of the Hopkins School, amid the terrors of the first Indian war, was taken out by night and left in the lonely cemetery. The next year Nathaniel Dickinson, Joseph Baldwin, Thomas Wells, and Richard Goodman, the latter killed by Indians while viewing his fences, were escorted to the graveyard by an armed guard and hastily interred. Parson Russell was called upon, in 1689, to mourn the death of his father, John Russell, Sr., and in 1681 the town lost Richard Montague, the grave-digger whose services as a baker for the soldiers when quartered in Hadley had saved them from starvation. Lieutenant Samuel Smith died in 1680, Andrew Warner and Robert Boltwood in 1684, and Philip Smith in 1685 met his death because of the practises of a witch. Samuel Porter, a strong supporter of the church, in 1698 rested from his labors in its behalf, and with Samuel Moody was laid beside his colleagues. One by one the old "engagers," Francis Barnard, Peter Tilton, William Markham, Timothy Nash, and Parson Russell himself, gave up their toils and struggles, until the close of the century found only Joseph Kellogg and John Hubbard living of those who built the first little homes on the broad street. A few years later every one of that valiant company except John White, William Lewis, John Marsh, William Goodwin, and John Crow, who had removed to other towns, were inhabitants of that silent settlement where wars and tumult were unknown.

No costly marble monuments mark the graves of those old first settlers, for they died in the midst of troubled times when care for the living was more important than unnecessary expense for the dead. A few rude gravestones were erected, some with figures carved upon their surfaces, and inscriptions which moss has overgrown and time obliterated. Slate stones were set up for those who died in later years, and after 1800 marble slabs were placed to mark the resting-places of those ancient worthies whose lives were their best monument. Many slaves were also buried in the old cemetery, but the rough stones on which were cut their names and virtues have long since crumbled away. No hearse was owned in Hadley until 1826. The path through the home lot of Edward Church was worn and beaten by the feet of the bearers as they passed in slow procession with the bier upon their shoulders to the place of burial. The minister stood among the neighbors who gathered round the grave, but no word was said and no prayers offered. Such were the funeral fashions of the fathers in colonial days.

The graves of three Hadley pioneers, Captain Aaron Cooke, Chileab Smith, and John Ingram, are marked with ancient headstones. The stone at the grave of Dr. John Westcarr, who died in 1675, seems to have been placed in position many years after his death. The old historian states that in 1858 there were only ten stones in the yard with dates earlier than

1720, and on many of these the inscription is now entirely obliterated. The oldest monuments in the cemetery are the sandstone tables erected in 1692 to the memory of Parson Russell and his wife, Rebekah. The inscription on the first, which is fully legible, reads as follows:

> REV RUSSELL'S REMAINS WHO FIRST GATHERED AND FOR 33 YEARS FAITHFULLY GOVERNED THE FLOCK OF CHRIST IN HADLEY TIL THE CHEIF SHEPHERD SUDDENLY BUT MERCIFULLY CALLED HIM OFF TO RECEIVE HIS REWARD IN THE 66 YEAR OF HIS AGE, DECEMBER 10, 1692.

The words above Rebekah declare:

> REBEKAH MADE BY GOD MEIT HELP TO MR JOHN RUSSELL AND FELLOW LABORER IN CHRIST'S WORK. A WISE VERTUOUS PIOUS MOTHER IN ISRAEL LYES HERE IN ASSURANCE OF A JOYFUL RESURRECTION. SHE DIED IN THE 57 YEAR OF HER AGE, NOVEMBER 21, 1688.

The graves of Rev. Isaac Chauncey and of Rev. Chester Williams are marked by upright sandstones, while a marble monument points out the place where lies Rev. Samuel Hopkins. Each of these stones bears an appropriate inscription describing the life and character of him who is buried beneath the stone. The cemetery was enlarged in 1828 and covers at present about four acres. Here, during all the years of its eventful history, the descendants of the first "engagers" have one by one returned to lay their friends and relatives by the side of the common ancestors, the founders of the town. Here is the newly made grave of Bishop Frederic D. Huntington, an illustrious son of Hadley, and every famous name of the old-time pioneers is repeated again and again on ancient and modern headstones.

No need is there to recite or emphasize the heroic deeds of each calm sleeper. The story is written in the history of the land which their sons and daughters have peopled with a race of men and women worthy of their sires.

INDEX

INDEX

A

Allis, William	4, 79
Amherst	50, 53, 91, 117
Amherst College	71, 94
Angel of Hadley, The	27
Army from Connecticut, The,	34
Ashfield	111
Attack on Hadley, The	35
Austin, Rev. Samuel	61
Ayres [Rev.] Roland	72

B

Bacon, Andrew	15, 118
Baldwin, Joseph	16, 119
Ball, Dyer	97
Barnard, Francis	16, 28, 119
John	78, 118
John, 2nd,	15, 16, 28
Joseph	21
Samuel	42, 45
Barnet, The	112
Barnstable	10
Bartlett, Daniel	66
Lyman	97
Bates, Isaac C	92
Bayne, Rev. J. S.	72
Beaman, Rev. Warren H.	72
Beecher, Henry Ward	97
Beers, Captain	25
Belding Samuel	4
Billing, Richard	4
Bloody Brook	28
Boardman, Rev. Daniel	81
Boltwood, Robert	16, 85, 119
Samuel	88
Bonney, Dr.	95
Boston, Joshua	48
Bradstreet, Simon	40
Branford	10
Breck, Rev. Robert	54
Bridgman, Elijah C.	97
Henry M.	97
James G.	97
Brown, Rev. John	72
Broom Industry, The	110
Burgoyne, General	64, 65

C

Chapin, John	106
Church, Benjamin	55
Edward	16, 117, 120
Richard	16, 42, 43, 118
Chauncey, Rev. Charles	41
Rev. Isaac	40, 43, 49, 121
Israel	53, 81
Nathaniel	81
Richard	50
Clark, Henry	16, 78, 118
William	12
Clary, John	88
Clinton, The	108
Coleman, John	4
Thomas	15, 118
Colt, Benjamin	62
Commissioners of the New England Colonies	28
Conway	111
Cook, Horace	96
Cooke, Aaron	10, 15, 31, 43, 46, 78, 87, 120

Cooke, Aaron, Jr. 25
    Moses 55, 89
    Noah 63
    Solomon 111
    Westwood 55, 89, 90, 101
Cowls, John 4, 62
Crow, John 16, 33, 84, 119
Cullick, John 77

D

Danforth, Francis 72
Davenport, John 77
Dedham 81
Deerfield 32, 53, 81
Dickinson, Azariah 26
    Benjamin 81
    Elijah 69
    Elisha 68, 89
    Hezekiah 44
    John 15, 32
    Levi 110, 111
    Nathaniel 2, 4, 8, 12, 14, 26, 78, 79, 119
        Nathaniel, Jr. 4
    Nehemiah 45
    Reuben 50
    Samuel 4
    Samuel, Dea. 89, 90
    Simeon 81
    Thomas 14
    William 92
Dispatch, The 108
Dunbar, John 97
Dwight, Daniel 81
    John 84
    Timothy 94
    Pres. Timothy 70
Dwight Memorial Library 84

E

Eastman, Joseph 89
Eaton, Gov. Theophilus 75, 77

Edwards, Jonathan 56, 57, 63
    Noah 106
Emmons, Rev. Nathaniel 61
Enfield Falls 112
Essex, England 8

F

Falls Boats 107
Falls Fight, The 32, 33
Fellows, Richard 4
Field, Zachariah 4
Flying Fish, The 108
Franklin, The 114

G

Gale, Levi 111
Gardner, Samuel 16
Gay, Ebenezer 81
Gaylord, Chester 92
    Nehemiah 66
    Samuel 56, 89
Goffe, General William 23, 31
Goodman, James 55
    John 15
    Richard 2, 5, 15, 30, 44, 119
Goodwin, William 11, 16, 77, 78, 82, 119
Grannis, Edward 21
Graves, Isaac 4, 12
    John, 4
    Thomas 4

H

Hampshire Troop, The 25
Harrison, Isaac 33
Hartford 1, 3, 4, 8, 31, 44, 76, 78, 81, 113
Harvard College 9, 41, 53, 79, 81, 90

Index

Harvard, John 75
Hatfield 4, 25, 26, 32, 54, 67, 81, 92, 96, 111
Hawkes, Gershom 36, 37
   John 16, 118
Hawley, Joseph 43, 87
Hooker, Rev. 61
   General Joseph 97
Hopkins, Gov. Edward 75, 76
   John 69
   Rev. Samuel 54, 57, 60, 67, 69, 121
Hopkins Academy 96
Hopkins Fund, The 78, 95
Hopkins Grammar School 79
Hovey, Thomas 89
Hubbard, Edmund 62, 89
   John 12, 15, 81, 119
   Joseph 55
Humphrey, President 71
Hunt, Ebenezer 70
Huntington, Rev. Dan 59, 92
   Rev. Frederic Dan 59, 122
   Theodore 96

I

Indian Fort, The 5, 79
Ingram, John 16, 120

J

James, John 81

K

Keedy, Rev. E. E. 72
Kellogg, Ezekiel 55
   Giles, Crouch 62, 92
   Joseph 7, 11, 14, 21, 31, 32, 34, 119

Kellogg, Joseph, Jr. 37, 55
Kelsey, Seymour 66
King Philip 24, 28, 36

L

Lake George, Battle of 59
Lamb, Daniel 106
Lewis, William 2, 15, 119
Lincoln, General 67
Locke, Dr. William 34
Longmeadow 57
Lothrop, Captain 25, 28, 34
Lyman, Enos 102
   Israel 68
   Rev. Joseph 67, 70, 92
   Phineas 62

M

Magnalia, The 38
Markham, William 3, 16, 119
Marsh, Daniel 45, 55
   Dwight, 97
   Ebenezer, 55, 62
   Job 55, 89, 90
   John 3, 16, 119
   Jonathan 46, 81
   Moses 55, 62, 63, 66, 67, 89
Martin, Rev. Benjamin 72
Mather, Cotton 38
   Nathaniel 81
   Prof. Richard H. 97
   Warham 81
Meekins, Thomas 4, 12
Montague, Peter 45
   Richard 7, 15, 20, 34, 119
Moody, Samuel 16, 40, 119
Morse, John 81
Muddy Brook 28

Index

N

Nash, Enos	57, 89
John	101
Rev. John A.	94
Josiah	66, 68
Samuel	37
Samuel	95
Newbury, Thomas	10
Timothy	16, 34, 119
New Haven	23, 70, 75, 94
New London	19, 111
Nichols, A.	16
George	94
Noble, Medad	66
Northampton	4, 5, 14, 17, 20, 25, 26, 32, 53, 56, 59, 61, 81, 90, 112
North Hadley	96
Norwalk	53
Norwich	33
Nye, Ichabod	66

P

Parsons, Rev. David	61, 70
Joseph	43
Partrigg, John	81
Samuel	34, 40, 43, 44, 81, 86
William	15, 118
Pease, Willis	113
Phelps, Charles	59, 67, 68, 89
Pierce, Josiah	62, 63, 84, 90, 102, 110
Pittsfield	111
Pixley, Wm.	16
Plummer, General Joseph B.	97
Pomeroy, Ebenezer	66
Titus	106
Pomfret	54
Porter, Aaron	81
Eleazer	46, 47, 48, 54, 63, 89, 112
Elisha	63, 64, 65, 89
Porter, Experience	97
Jeremiah	55
Jonathan Edwards	64
Moses	56, 58, 60, 68, 69, 92
Samuel	15, 34
Samuel, 2nd	43, 44, 45, 46, 63, 67, 68, 89, 92, 119
Samuel, 3d	55
Prentice, John	19
Proprietors of the Locks and Canals	109
Prutt, Arthur	49
Zebulon	51
Pynchon, John	1, 2, 20, 24, 28, 43, 87

R

Rand, Rev. William	53
Reed, Thomas	30, 32
Regicides, The	22
Riddle, Rev. William	61
Rugg, Samuel	101
Russell, Rev. Ezekiel	94
John	3, 14, 19
Parson John	1, 3, 10, 11, 15, 17, 19, 21, 22, 29, 31, 34, 39, 40, 75, 78, 86, 97, 119, 121
Jonathan	10
Philip	9
Samuel	10
Russell Church, The	71

S

Saratoga, Battle of	64
Seelye, Pres. L. Clark	97
Slavery in Hadley	48
Shays, Daniel	67
Shepherd, Levi	106
Shipman, William	111
Smith, Benjamin	88

Index

Smith Caleb	68, 88
Chileab, 1st	16, 120
Chileab, 2nd	46, 89
David	89
Dudley	65
Ebenezer	42
Eliakim	56, 62
Enos	58, 67
Erastus	88
Ichabod	55
Jacob	71, 92
John, Dea.	46, 55, 89
John	90
Joseph	81, 89
Noah	63
Oliver	62, 66, 89
Percy	68
Philip	15, 31, 37, 38, 86, 117, 119
Rodney	84
Samuel	3, 4, 6, 12, 15, 17, 25, 30, 65, 78, 117, 119
Seth	92
Timothy	66
Warham	63
Windsor	68
Rev. Worthington	94
Smith College	97
South Hadley	52, 90
South Hadley Falls	102, 109
Springfield	12, 25, 28, 32, 54, 94
Standley, Thomas	4, 7
Stanley, Nathaniel	15
Thomas	4, 7, 15, 118
Steele, Stephen	81
Stockbridge, Levi	96, 97
Stratford	41
Strong, Governor	60, 70
Sunderland	53
Swan, Thomas	81

T

Taylor, John	16
Taylor, Oliver S.	94
Stephen	4
Terry, Stephen	16, 118
Tilton, Peter	6, 15, 23, 31, 78, 83, 119
Traynor, Francis	66
Treat, Salmon	81
Turner, William	32

U

United Colonies of New England	76
Utrecht	44 58

V

Vermont, The	108, 113
Vermont, University of	94

W

Ward, Nathaniel	2, 5, 16, 78, 79, 82, 118
Warner, Andrew	16, 44, 79, 119
Daniel	4
Jonathan	62
Oliver	52, 55
Orange	45
Warren, Lemuel	68
Watson, Caleb	79
Webster, Gov. John	3, 16, 19, 117
Mary	15, 37
Noah	117
Wells, Jonathan	33
Thomas	12, 15, 119
Thomas, Jr.	21
Westcarr, Dr. John	20, 21, 120
Westfield	3, 32
West Springfield	57
Westwood, William	2, 4, 7, 10, 12, 15, 118

Wethersfield 1, 4, 8, 9, 81, 110	
Whalley, Gen. Edward 23, 24	
White, Daniel 4, 67	
John 2, 4, 15, 119	
John, Jr. 4	
Nathaniel 46, 67	
Whitefield, Rev. George 54	
Whiting, Rev. John 10	
Whitney, Prof. William D 97	
William Hall, The 113	
Williams, Rev. Chester 54, 56, 121	
Rev. Ebenezer 54	
Elisha 81	
Rev. John 53	
Solomon 81	
Williams, Rev. Stephen 57, 81
Williamsburg 111
Windsor 3, 10, 15, 81
Witchcraft in Hadley 37
Woburn 90
Woodbridge, Rev. John 69, 92
Worcester, Rev. Leonard 61

Y

Yale, David 76
  Elihu 76
Yale College 54, 57, 72, 81, 97
Younglove, John 80

www.ingramcontent.com/pod-product-compliance
Lightning Source LLC
Chambersburg PA
CBHW071721090426
42738CB00009B/1839